16x's 5/07

D1192176

CANADA

A PRIMARY SOURCE CULTURAL GUIDE

Lois Sakany

The Rosen Publishing Group's
PowerPlus Books™
New York

To my son, Isaiah

Published in 2004 by The Rosen Publishing Group, Inc.
29 East 21st Street, New York, NY 10010

Copyright © 2004 by The Rosen Publishing Group, Inc.

First Edition

All rights reserved. No part of this book may be reproduced in any form without permission in writing from the publisher, except by a reviewer.

Library of Congress Cataloging-in-Publication Data
Sakany, Lois.
Canada : a primary source cultural guide / Lois Sakany.— 1st ed.
    p. cm. — (Primary sources of world cultures)
Summary: An overview of the history and culture of Canada and its people including the geography, myths, arts, daily life, education, industry, and government, with illustrations from primary source documents.
Includes bibliographical references and index.
ISBN 0-8239-3998-7 (library binding)
1. Canada—Civilization—Juvenile literature. 2. Canada—Civilization—Sources—Juvenile literature. [1. Canada.]
I. Title. II. Series.
F1021.S25 2004
971—dc21

2003002203

Manufactured in the United States of America

Cover images (clockwise from left): A seventeenth-century map of New France as drawn by Samuel de Champlain; the Canadian Parliament building in Ottawa, Ontario; and a Canadian Mountie on horseback.

Photo credits: cover (background), pp. 27, 28 (top and bottom), 29 (bottom), 83, 116 (right) © Hulton Archive/Getty Images; cover (middle), p. 44 © Gunter Max Photography/Corbis; cover (bottom), pp. 5 (middle), 38, 39, 42 (top), 43, 58, 74, 80, 81, 82, 92, 100 (bottom), 106, 111 (top and bottom) © Matton Images; pp. 3, 118, 120 © 2002 GeoAtlas; pp. 4 (top), 8, 118 (bottom left) © Brian Yarvin/Photo Researchers, Inc.; pp. 4 (middle), 31 © Robert Harris/National Archives of Canada/C-002149; pp. 4 (bottom), 5 (bottom), 11, 40, 41, 53, 54, 55, 56, 57 (bottom), 97 (top), 98, 99, 100 (top), 101, 102, 104, 108, 109 (top), 110 © Megapress Images Inc.; pp. 5 (top), 70 © Nicolas Sapieha/Art Archive; pp. 6, 14, 37, 71, 94 © B&C Alexander/Photo Researchers, Inc.; p. 7 © Lionel F. Stevenson/Photo Researchers, Inc.; p. 9 © F. Jourdan/Explorer/ Photo Researchers, Inc.; p. 10 © Georg Gerster/Dupe/Photo Researchers, Inc.; p. 12 © Adam Jones/Photo Researchers, Inc.; p. 15 © Andrew J. Martinez/Photo Researchers, Inc.; p. 16 © Raymond Gehman/Corbis; p. 17 © John Serrao/Photo Researchers, Inc.; p. 18 © P. Renault/Photo Researchers, Inc.; p. 19 © Paul A. Souders/Corbis; p. 20 © Larose/RÈflexion/Megapress Images Inc.; p. 22 © Robert Estall/Corbis; p. 23 © Jonathan Blair/Corbis; p. 24 © Brian A. Vikander/Corbis; p. 25 © Dagli Orti/Navy Historical Service Vincennes France/Art Archive; pp. 26, 116 (left) © Library of Congress, Washington, D.C., USA/Bridgeman Art Library/Superstock; p. 29 (top) © Dagli Orti/Bibliotheque des Arts Decoratifs Paris/Art Archive; pp. 30, 61, 62 (bottom), 63 © Bettmann/Corbis; p. 33 (top and bottom) © Canadian Pacific Railroad Archive; p. 34 (top) © Hulton-Deutsch Collection/Corbis; p. 34 (bottom) © Dagli Orti/Musee des 2 Guerres Mondiales Paris/Art Archive; p. 35 (top) © William C. Shrout/TimePix; p. 35 (bottom) © Imperial War Museum/Art Archive; p. 36 © Robert Cooper/National Archives of Canada/ PA-141503; p. 42 (bottom) © Helen Marcus/Photo Researchers, Inc.; pp. 45, 46, 47 © Peter Harholdt/Corbis; pp. 48, 50 © The Granger Collection; pp. 52, 88 © Mike Blake/Reuters/Getty Images; p. 57 (top) © Shaun Best/Reuters/Getty Images; pp. 59, 60 © Werner Forman/ Corbis; p. 62 (top) © Dagli Orti/Private Collection/Art Archive; p. 64 © Bridgeman Art Library, London/Superstock; p. 65 © Perry Mastrovito/ Corbis; p. 66 © Richard A. Cooke/Corbis; p. 67 © Roger Ressmeyer/Corbis; p. 68 © Annie Griffiths Belt/Corbis; p. 69, 78 © Michael S. Yamashita/Corbis; p. 72 © Porterfield/Chickering/Photo Researchers, Inc.; p. 73 © Dewitt Jones/Corbis; pp. 75, 118 (top) © Will & Deni McIntyre/Photo Researchers, Inc.; pp. 77, 79, 118 (bottom right) © Tony Stone/Getty Images; p. 84 © Carolyn Djanogly/Aurora Photos; p. 85 © Christopher J. Morris/Corbis; p. 86 © Pierre-Paul Poulin/Magma; p. 87 © Reuters NewMedia, Inc./Corbis; p. 89 © Julie Lemberger/ Corbis; p. 90 © AFP/Corbis; p. 91 © Mitchell Gerber/Corbis; p. 93 © Jeff Greenberg/Photo Researchers, Inc.; pp. 95, 107 © Jeff Epstein; p. 96 © E. Brenckle/Explorer/Photo Researchers, Inc.; p. 97 (bottom) © John Eastcott/Yva Momatiuk/Photo Researchers, Inc.; p. 105 © Kevin R. Morris/Corbis; p. 109 (bottom) © Jim Young/Reuters/Getty Images.

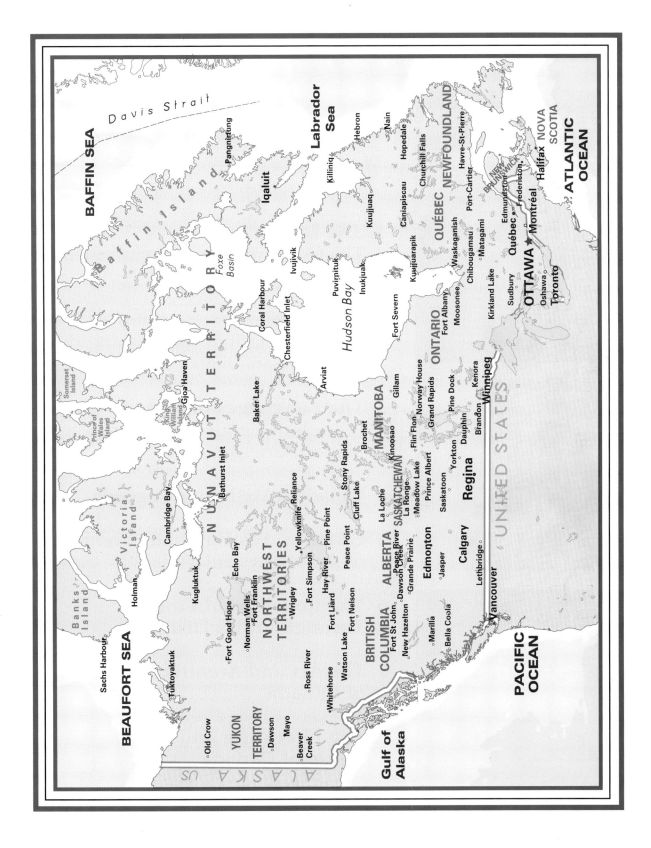

CONTENTS

INTRODUCTION

C anada is one of the largest countries in the world, second in size only to Russia. The vastness of its land has had a major influence on its overall development. Thousands of years ago, Canada's first people traveled there as explorers and then chose it as a place to settle because of its abundant natural resources. European explorers also came and remained because Canada and the oceans that surrounded it were so rich with fish and animal life.

Canada's great size means more than a wealth of natural resources, however. With seemingly endless room to grow, Canadians have always allowed space for other cultures. When England defeated France in the Seven Years' War, French Canadians were able to hold on to their culture and to this day exert a major influence on Canadian language (the official languages of Canada are French and English), culture, and politics. In recent years, Canada has even seen fit to make some reparations to Canada's first explorers in the form of Nunavut, a new territory, which is self-governed by the Inuit First Nations.

Canada's great size and largely inhospitable terrain have made development slow at times.

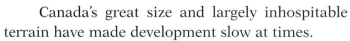

Cotton grass covers Ellesmere National Park Reserve *(left)* in a small area near Lake Hazen, which is especially lush due to the melted glacial waters that feed its vegetation. Elsewhere in the park the landscape is largely composed of rock and ice. It is a polar desert that is one of the driest regions in the Northern Hemisphere. Because of the low temperatures, there is little flora or fauna in this section of Canada. This church *(above)*, located at Prince Edward Island, is situated in the Gulf of Saint Lawrence off the Atlantic coast of mainland Canada, an area rich with wetlands, woodlands, and farms.

Located in British Columbia, Vancouver is nestled between the snow-capped Coast Mountain Range and the Fraser River approximately 24 miles (38 kilometers) north of the Canada–United States border. The weather in Vancouver is the mildest in Canada, in part because of warm Pacific Ocean currents that originate near Japan. The name "Vancouver" may have originated from Captain George Vancouver, whose ancestors came from the Dutch town of Van Coeverden, a name that means "cow crossing."

Seeking out the country's most temperate regions, 90 percent of Canadians live within 300 miles (483 kilometers) of the southern border. There, Canadians are often more bombarded by the economy and culture of their neighbors to the south, the Americans, than they are by Canadian neighbors who might live five time zones, two mountain ranges, and thousands of miles away.

Despite these challenges, or perhaps because of them, Canada has developed a strong national identity. This identity is recognized internationally for its blending of a myriad of economic, political, and social influences. And while Canadians may often feel separated by geography, they are united in their belief that a strong Canada is one that respects its roots while still remaining open to change.

At the start of the new millennium, Canadians have much of which to be proud. Canada possesses an economy that is both strong and stable,

Québec, with its 205.1 million acres (83.9 million hectares) of forest, is the cornerstone of the Canadian forest industry. The three main types of forest in this region are the boreal, mixed wood, and hardwood. The Canadian government, both at the local and national level, monitors the forestry industry to ensure and maintain its growth.

and while there are still political differences between French and English Canada, the country remains united, while still preserving unique aspects of both cultures. Canada boasts a long list of fine artists, authors, and performers who are well known internationally and viewed as being distinctly Canadian. Canada has flourished as a nation with a combination of grace and practicality.

THE LAND

The Geography and Environment of Canada

S panning the continent of North America as well as six time zones, Canada is bordered by the Atlantic Ocean on the east coast, the Pacific Ocean on the west coast, and the Arctic Ocean to the north. Canada's coastlines stretch some 146,000 miles (234,964 kilometers). To its south and northwest, Canada shares the world's largest international boundary with its only land neighbor, the United States. The border between Canada and the United States is 5,335 miles (8,585 kilometers) long.

In western Canada, the Coast Mountains and Rocky Mountains combine to form a beautiful, jagged landscape. East of the Rocky Mountains, a wide expanse of flat land, interrupted only by the low Laurentian Mountains in Québec and the Appalachian Mountains along the East Coast, reaches toward the Atlantic Ocean. Canada shares Lakes Superior, Huron, Erie, and Ontario with the United States. Canada's major rivers are the Churchill, Fraser, Mackenzie, Nelson, and the Saint Lawrence.

The country is divided into ten provinces and three northern territories. The provinces, lying east to west, are Newfoundland, Nova Scotia, Prince Edward Island, New Brunswick, Québec, Ontario, Manitoba, Saskatchewan, Alberta, and British Columbia. The Northwest Territories, the Nunavut

The Victoria Bridge in Montréal *(left)* crosses the St. Lawrence River, a freshwater river that stretches 1,900 miles (3,058 kilometers) beginning at Lake Ontario. Before it empties into the Atlantic Ocean at the Gulf of St. Lawrence, it passes through two of Canada's largest cities, Montréal and Québec. The St. Lawrence River serves as an important source of hydroelectric power for Canada. The Badlands Formation *(above)* is part of Dinosaur Provincial Park in Alberta. This rich geological formation was created about 75 million years ago and harbors a succession of rock layers in which paleontologists have found the bones of more than forty specimens of dinosaurs and 500 intact skeletons.

The Canadian Rocky Mountains are part of the Rocky Mountain chain, which stretches from Alaska to New Mexico and crosses two countries, one territory, two provinces, and six states. Although the weather in the Canadian Rocky Mountains can be unpredictable because of the high elevation and rugged topography, these mountains provide an array of adventure activities, such as fishing, backpacking, mountain climbing, and horse pack trips. The Canadian Rockies are also a vast ecosystem of indigenous wildlife, including species such as the wolf and mountain sheep.

Territory, and the Yukon Territory, lie to the north. Though Canada is quite large, its rugged topography and severe climate combine to make it one of the least densely populated countries in the world. There are roughly 30 million people living in Canada, and 75 percent of the population lives within one hundred miles (150 kilometers) of the country's southern border. As one moves farther north, the winters become harsh and the land becomes all but uninhabitable by humans. However, this northern wilderness is rich in natural resources. Canada is the world's largest exporter of forest products and a top exporter of fish, furs, and wheat.

Topography

Canada is not only vast in size, but it is also varied in topography. The country is divided into seven major topographical regions. Each region encompasses provinces or areas of land that share certain environmental traits, such as elevation, vegetation, and climate. The seven regions are known as the Western Cordillera, the Arctic Lowlands and the Arctic Islands, the Interior Plains, the Canadian Shield, the Hudson Bay Lowlands, the Great Lakes and the St. Lawrence Lowlands, and the Appalachian Regions.

The Western Cordillera

The Western Cordillera is a vast system of mountain chains, steep valleys, and plateaus that extend along the length of the Pacific Coast of North and South America. These steep mountain chains were formed approximately 80 million years ago, during a period of dramatic geological change. The crust of Earth is broken into large pieces, which are known as plates. About 80 million years ago, the Pacific plate was driven under the North American plate, forcing the land to buckle and bend, creating the jagged peaks of the coastal mountain ranges.

The Pacific Range, which is a part of the Western Cordillera, forms Canada's westernmost land region. Canada's highest mountain peak, St. Elias, is part of the Pacific Range and is located in the Yukon Territory near the Alaskan border. It rises 19,524 feet (5,951 meters) above sea level. The Pacific Range dominates the landscape of British Columbia and the southwestern portion of the Yukon Territory. It extends into the Pacific Ocean, where only its tallest peaks can be seen above water. Queen Charlotte Island and Vancouver Island, both located off the coast of British Columbia, are the peaks of mountains otherwise hidden under the cold waters of the northern Pacific Ocean.

The Rocky Mountains add to the grandeur of the Western Cordillera as well. The Rocky Mountains extend for more than three thousand miles (4,800 kilometers) from northern Alaska to New Mexico. The Rocky Mountain Range is divided into five regions. These regions, lying from north to south, are known as the Brooks Range, the Canadian Rockies, the Northern Rockies, the Middle Rockies, and the Southern Rockies. The largest mountains within the chain are the Canadian Rockies. Running north to south just east of the Pacific Range along the border between British Columbia and Alberta, the Canadian Rockies vary in height from seven thousand feet to more than twelve thousand feet (2,100 to 3,660 meters) above sea level.

Though the Western Cordillera mountain chains are sparsely populated, they are immensely popular among Canadians. Naturalists and nature lovers flock to the region to experience the magnificent scenery and to enjoy outdoor activities, including hiking, boating, camping, and skiing.

Inuit shoppers in this photograph pay a visit to the Hudson Bay Company store. The Inuit, once known as Eskimos, inhabit lands from the northeastern tip of Russia, across Alaska to northern Canada, to parts of Greenland. As they moved eastward, they adapted to the cold, harsh Arctic terrain, though they have largely abandoned their traditional way of life. These people, who once lived in igloos, wore animal skin garments, and traveled by dogsled, now inhabit wooden houses, wear modern clothing, travel by snowmobiles, and speak English, Russian, or Danish in addition to their native language. They maintain connections to their heritage through oral storytelling, music, dancing, and arts and crafts.

The Arctic Lowlands and the Arctic Islands

The Arctic Lowlands dominate the northern portion of the Northwest Territories. This region is cold, isolated from the large cities to the south, and almost entirely uninhabited. The exceptions are the widely scattered Inuit and Dene communities, both members of Canada's native population, who struggled for many years to defend their claims to the land. In 1999, these native peoples voted to create a new territory, known as Nunavut, from the eastern reaches of the Northwest Territories. Nunavut is dominated by the Inuit, while the Dene dominate the western regions of the Northwest Territories.

Directly north of the Arctic Lowlands are the Artic Islands. They are almost entirely within the Arctic Circle, the imaginary circle that circles Earth at a latitude of 66.5 degrees north. The Arctic Islands are composed of a dozen large islands and hundreds of smaller ones. All of the islands are barren and most remain unexplored. Two of the largest islands, Baffin Island and Ellesmere Island, are covered with mountains, glaciers, and fjords, which are ocean inlets bordered by steep cliffs.

Both the Arctic Lowlands and the Arctic Islands are tundra, which are wide plains too cold and too dry for trees to grow. On the tundra, the subsoil is permanently frozen. Only a thin surface layer of soil thaws during the brief, cool summers, allowing mosses, lichens, and sedges to grow in abundance. In midwinter, the sun is visible for only a few hours per day, while in midsummer, it shines almost twenty-four hours per day.

The Interior Plains

The plains dominate North America's interior from the southern United States to the arctic tundra of northern Canada. Within Canada, this region encompasses much of the central provinces of Alberta, Saskatchewan, and the southern part of Manitoba. The Interior Plains are bound on the west by the Canadian Rockies and on the east by the Canadian Shield.

Once a vast prairie and home to large herds of buffalo, the Interior Plains have been transformed into farmland dominated by the production of grains, including wheat, oilseed, canola, soy, and barley. Wheat is the most commonly farmed grain, giving the region its reputation as Canada's breadbasket.

American bison, more commonly known as buffalo, are the largest mammals on the North American continent. They inhabit areas where there is adequate forage, water, and space, namely in parks in the western United States and Northwest Territories of Canada. Today, about 65,000 bison live in national parks and on reserves.

The Canadian Shield is 3,000,000 square miles (8,000,000 square kilometers) in area. Although its harsh climate and terrain make it largely inhospitable, there is still a population of Inuit living in the area. Its primary industries are farming, mining, and forestry. In 1989, diamonds were discovered in the Northwest Territories. Until that time, South Africa was the only country to have gem-sized diamonds.

The Canadian Shield

The Canadian Shield is a vast horseshoe-shaped region that curves around Hudson Bay from the Arctic coast to the Newfoundland coast of Labrador. The region covers about half of the country's land-mass. Mountains once covered the area known today as the Canadian Shield. Over the course of millions of years, glacial erosion wore down the steep mountain peaks. Today, the region is marked by low hills and is covered by forests and the count-less lakes that feed the nation's waterways. The soil is rich in minerals such as iron and nickel. The area is a favorite destination of fishers and hunters. Residents of Toronto, Ottawa, and Montréal often vacation at lake or mountain resorts located along the southern edge of the Canadian Shield. However, because the soil is not good for farming and the climate is cold, the region is largely uninhabited by permanent residents

The Canadian Shield dominates the Canadian landscape. This dominance has in many ways shaped Canada's development as a country. The region's rugged topog-raphy has discouraged settlement, which explains why most of Canada's population lives along the southern border. In addition, the Canadian Shield separates the major cities of the east and west coast. The result has been not only physical isolation but at times a political, social, and cultural division as well.

The Hudson Bay Lowlands

The Hudson Bay Lowlands are a flat, swampy region located between the Canadian Shield and the southwestern coast of Hudson Bay. Combined with the Hudson Strait Basin, the Hudson Bay Lowlands cover about one-third of mainland Canada. The

largest river in this basin is the Nelson River, which flows from Lake Winnipeg to Hudson Bay.

The Great Lakes and the St. Lawrence Lowlands

The Great Lakes and the St. Lawrence Lowlands regions encompass the rolling countryside along the St. Lawrence River and the peninsula of southern Ontario. It is one of the most fertile and temperate areas in Canada, and as a result, it is also the location of the country's largest metropolitan centers. These cities include Montréal, Québec City, Toronto, and Ottawa. This part of eastern Canada contains more large cities with populations of more than one hundred thousand people than any other part of Canada of a similar size.

The Canadian Shield, the largest exposed mass of Precambrian rocks, was formed when two tectonic plates converged, causing the surface rock to be forced under into the interior of the earth, where it melted before rising slowly to the earth's surface. This photograph, taken in the Canadian Shield, shows Precambrian Era shield rocks near Manitoba. The Precambrian Era is one of the major divisions of geological time that occurred from 5 billion to 570 million years ago.

The Great Lakes and the St. Lawrence Lowlands are the country's industrial heartland. Seventy-five percent of the country's manufactured goods are produced in the region. Industry dominates the Québec-Windsor corridor, an area that stretches between Québec and Windsor along the shores of the St. Lawrence River and Lake Ontario. In addition, by making good use of the fertile soil and a cooperative climate, farmers in the area produce about one-third of Canada's agricultural output.

The Appalachian Region

Named for the Appalachian Mountains, the Appalachian Region includes southeastern Québec and most of the Atlantic Provinces. The Appalachian Mountain Range is an ancient collection of mountains that extend from the Canadian island of Newfoundland to the state of Alabama. Low mountains and thick forests characterize the chain. In Canada, the range's highest peaks can be found on the Gaspé Peninsula of Québec, where the Shickshock Mountains are located. These mountains reach just higher than four thousand feet (1,220 meters) above sea level.

Only a small percentage of Canadians live in this region, which has long been the poorest section of Canada. The main industries are dependent on resources such as fish and timber.

Natural Resources

Canada is a country of bountiful natural resources. The majority of the country's wealth comes from developing or harvesting natural resources, such as trees, fish, oil, natural

This paper factory in Québec is just one of many businesses that make up the Canadian paper and pulp industry, the backbone of the Canadian economy. The export-driven forest industry employs more than one million people with four out of five tons of paper exported annually. The forestry industry also maintains the forests and ecosystems in Canada, investing billions of dollars into recycling programs that produce high quality recycled paper products.

gas, minerals, and water. The United States is Canada's most reliable customer for these and other natural resources.

Canada is the world's largest exporter of forest products, including timber, wood pulp, and paper. The national and provincial governments own most of the forests and lease them to private companies. British Columbia, Québec, and Ontario lead the provinces in timber production. More than a million Canadians have jobs that are dependent on the forestry industry.

The fishing industry is also important to the Canadian economy, and the Grand Banks, located off the coast of Newfoundland, have long ranked among the world's best fishing grounds. Today, the major products of Canada's Atlantic waters include a wide variety of fish and shellfish, especially crab and lobster. On the Pacific coast, fishermen harvest salmon, halibut, and herring. Fishing fleets catch most of the

The mining equipment in this photograph is at the bottom of the Highland Copper Mine in British Columbia, an open pit nearly 1,000 feet (305 meters) deep. It is the largest mine of its kind in North America and is one of the few human-engineered projects visible from the moon. More than 90 million tons of ore per year are extracted from its core. The first record of copper in Canada was reported in the accounts of Samuel de Champlain in 1604 in an area called Gaspé, which was eventually developed into a mine. The search for valuable metals and minerals contributed to the settlement of remote areas of Canada, a nation that now produces sixty kinds of metals and minerals, including gold, copper, iron ore, zinc, and nickel.

The Daniel Johnson Dam in Côte-Nord (above) provides hydroelectric power. Named after a former Québec premier who helped develop hydroelectricity, the Daniel Johnson Dam is the largest hollow-body, multiple arch dam in the world. Its nickname is Manic 5. This refers to the Manicougan River, which provides electricity to the eastern seaboard of Canada and the United States.

salmon near the mouths of major rivers in British Columbia. However, fish species on both coasts are being depleted at an alarming rate in order to meet the demands of international consumers, and the industry faces serious natural threats.

Canada is also rich in minerals, which has played an important role in the country's industrial economy. The provinces of Alberta, British Columbia, Québec, and Saskatchewan are the principal mining regions. Ontario, the Northwest Territories, and the Yukon Territory are also significant producers. Canada is one of the leading exporters of a wide variety of minerals, including copper, gold, iron, nickel, potash, uranium, and zinc.

Petroleum and natural gas are two of Canada's valuable mined products, and petroleum is now one of Canada's main exports. Large reserves of petroleum are thought to exist in the Arctic, but the ruggedness of the terrain makes access to these sources prohibitively expensive. The majority of the petroleum and natural gas that Canada exports is found in Alberta, Saskatchewan, and Manitoba, and most of it is sold to the United States.

Close to 10 percent of Canada's land is devoted to agricultural production, which is dominated by wheat, beef cattle, dairy, and hogs. The majority of Canada's wheat is grown in Saskatchewan, and a large percentage is farmed in Alberta and Manitoba. Livestock, including beef cattle, dairy cattle, hogs, and poultry, is generally raised on farms in Alberta.

Canada is filled with fast-flowing rivers, and the country has used their strength to become one of the world's leading producers of hydroelectric power. Though petroleum products are the number one source of energy for Canadians, hydroelectric energy is also a significant contributor, in addition to nuclear power and coal.

Climate

Canada's proximity to the southern reaches of the Arctic Circle accounts for its climate, which ranges from extremely cold in the north to cool in the south. Chilled by Arctic winds from the west, most of the country experiences average winter temperatures below 0°F (-8°C). The average temperature is predictably much more severe in the Arctic regions, where much of the land is permanently frozen. Like the northwestern United States, the coastal regions of British Columbia are warmed by the northeasterly currents of the Pacific Ocean. These regions experience milder winters and a high level of precipitation. The annual rainfall regularly exceeds 100 inches (250 centimeters), and most of this precipitation falls in the autumn and winter.

Summer in northern Canada is short and cool. In the Arctic Islands, temperatures in July average below 40°F (4°C). Closer to the southern border, summers are long and warm enough to raise crops. The plains regions, as in the United States, experience greater temperature fluctuations. There, extremely cold winters are often followed by hot and dry summers. Closer to the coasts, the oceans make the climate more temperate, so the shifts in climate from season to season are not as severe.

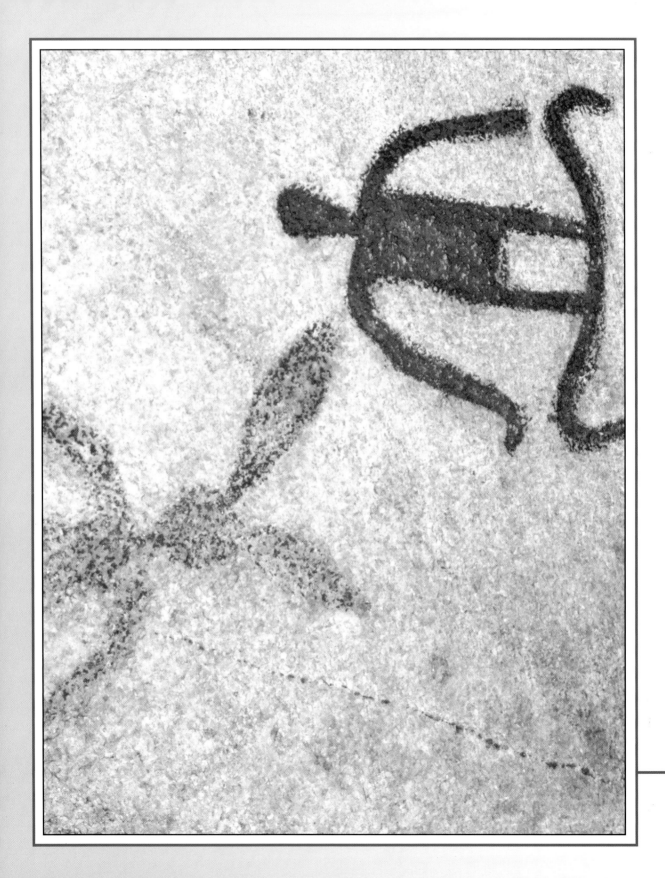

THE PEOPLE

2

The Ancient First Nations and the Modern Canadians

L ong before Canada existed as a nation, it was settled by the Paleo-Indians. Many experts believe this group first came to live in the Americas toward the end of the Ice Age, or approximately fifteen thousand years ago. The most widely accepted theory tells us that the Paleo-Indians reached North America by traveling across a land bridge known as Beringia. Now submerged by the Bering Sea, Beringia once stretched fifty miles (eighty kilometers) between modern-day Siberia and Alaska.

The first evidence of human habitation in Canada consists of the tools they left behind. Scientists have determined that these artifacts date from between 9500 and 8000 BC. There is archaeological evidence that these groups traded with one another but were otherwise isolated and self-sufficient.

As the Ice Age ended and the glaciers that covered the continent retreated north and east, settlers spread farther east in search of more favorable hunting and fishing sites. To those first people, all of North America was endless frontier. Their greatest challenges came not from confrontations with other people but from steep mountains, wide rivers, and wild animals.

These Algonquin petroglyphs *(left)* were cut into marble and found in Peterborough, Ontario. Archaeologists believe that Algonquin-speaking aboriginal people carved the petroglyphs 500 to 1,000 years ago. They are thought to be portrayals of the human relationship with the spirit world. A fossil of the extinct lobe-finned fish miguasha *(above)* is one of the most studied in the world. Its strong spine and bony, even-numbered fin structure gave way to the emergence of tetrapods—four-legged, air-breathing terrestrial vertebrates. These fish inhabited what is now Québec's Gaspé Peninsula 370 million years ago when it was a tropical estuary.

The Thule, ancient ancestors of the Inuit, built these stone traps around AD 900 to capture bears and wolves. The Thule were whalers of northern Alaska who migrated eastward to Canada, probably following the migration of the mammals. When they arrived in Canada, they found other resources to sustain them, such as bear, caribou, walrus, and wolf. One major contribution of the Thule was that of the dogsled. The first appearance of dog harnesses and equipment for dog traction were found in Canadian Thule settlements.

Over the next several thousand years, though exploration continued, various groups settled and created permanent communities, coming together for protection. Fossil evidence from these settlements suggests that they enjoyed both a temperate climate and abundant natural resources. On the western plains, scientists have found evidence of a community organized around communal bison hunting. By 1000 BC, there were permanent coastal settlements that depended on shellfish harvested from the sea.

Cultural Advancements

Around this time, two remarkable inventions, the bow and the clay pot, quickly spread across North America. These advances changed how wildlife was hunted and how food was prepared and stored. The rapid spread of this new technology indicates that there was a substantial amount of trade among the people. These inventions spurred others, and the communities prospered.

There is evidence that during this period people in certain regions of Canada also began to cultivate plants. The practice began in Mexico and spread northward along the Mississippi River until it was first practiced in present-day Ontario.

Though it is difficult to make accurate estimates, researchers believe that anywhere from 250,000 to 500,000 indigenous, or native, people lived in Canada when the first European adventurers, missionaries, and traders arrived in the late fifteenth century. The largest of these groups were located where the climate was more temperate.

A Inuit man, a native of Prince Regent's Bay, appeared in the *Travels of Sir John Ross*. Sir John Ross was an English explorer searching for the Northwest Passage. He discovered Baffin Bay, the Gulf of Boothia, and King William Island. During an expedition in 1829, Ross and his crew were forced to spend the harsh Canadian winter on land. During that time, they were visited by the Inuit, who drew maps of the surrounding area indicating to Ross that they were on the mainland of North America.

Ervick a Native of Prince Regents Bay

Diverse Peoples

Among Canada's indigenous people, who are also known as the First Nations, there were at least twelve major linguistic families. The largest groups of these were the Athabascan of the west and north, and the Algonquin, who dominated the east. The Algonquin hunted deer, moose, caribou, seals, and walruses and used their hides, meat, and bones for food, clothing, and tools. They gathered wild rice and an assortment of berries, nuts, and plants. The frozen north was occupied by the Inuit, who were among the second wave of immigrants who arrived in North America. In the winter, the Inuit lived in frozen huts called igloos, and in the summer, they lived in tents made of animal skin. They were well known for their skill in making weapons and tools.

The Iroquois are known to have settled in southern Ontario and along the St. Lawrence River. Soon they evolved from hunters into a seminomadic and agricultural people. This means that they moved every ten to fifteen years when the fertility of the soil they farmed became exhausted. When they found rich soil, they established villages. They constructed homes that were up to sixty yards long and twelve yards wide. These "longhouses" were occupied by a single clan, which was made up of ten to thirty related families who shared a single matriarch, or female ancestor. Several clans grouped together formed a tribe. By the late fifteenth century, the Iroquois had developed a political, social, and cultural organization known as the Five Nations, or the Iroquois Confederacy. The confederacy was governed by a council of fifty permanent chiefs, who voted on important issues affecting the member nations.

This nineteenth-century painting depicts Leif Eriksson discovering North America. During the winter of AD 1001, Eriksson landed on the continent and he and his men built houses. They found the ground frost-free and agreed that fodder and other food for animals, which would normally be kept during harsh winters, were not needed. The rivers and lakes were plentiful with fish, and the earth was rich for growing crops. It was so fertile that Eriksson called it "Vinland the Good."

Norsemen: The First Europeans

In the late tenth and early eleventh centuries, Scandinavian mariners, known as Norsemen or Vikings, explored the Atlantic in search of undiscovered lands. These mariners colonized Iceland and then Greenland. During this time, the ship of a Norseman by the name of Bjarni Herjolfsson was blown off course while traveling from Iceland to Greenland. The ship reportedly reached the coast of Labrador, but Herjolfsson chose not to explore the irregular coastline because, from his view at sea, the land appeared barren and inhospitable.

Leif Eriksson, another Norseman, was the first European to set foot on North American soil. Based on his descriptions, historians believe that he probably landed on or near the northern coast of Labrador. On later voyages, Eriksson visited a region he called Vinland. Historians have long debated Vinland's location, which is thought to be a site along the Atlantic coast.

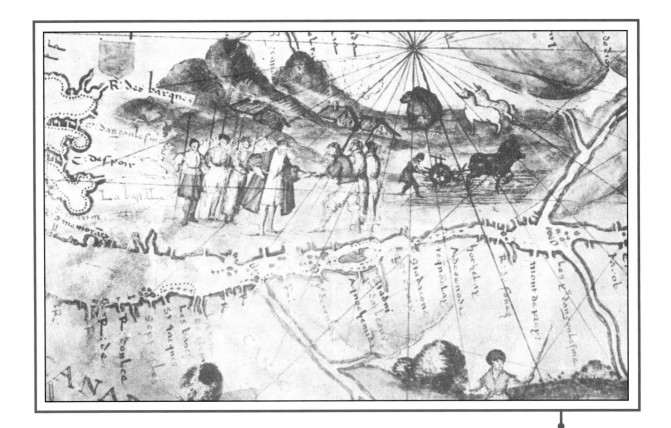

Though the location of Vinland remains a mystery, historians believe that it was rich in natural resources. The Norsemen attempted to establish permanent settlements at Vinland for years. In response to the European invasion of their land, the native population fought any attempts they made to settle. In one battle, Eriksson's brother was killed. Eventually the Norsemen were driven back to Greenland. However, trade between the native peoples and the Norsemen continued until approximately the fourteenth century.

This historic map of Canada shows the St. Lawrence River and a group of men under the direction of French navigator Jacques Cartier. Remembered as the explorer of the St. Lawrence, Cartier made three expeditions to the area beginning in 1534. He kept detailed records of his expeditions, and his accounts are the first reliable documentation of European exploration in North America.

The English and the French

Interest in exploring the New World waned with the Norsemen's abandonment of their settlements, and by the time Christopher Columbus set sail in search of a faster trade route to China, the details of the Norsemen's visit were lost to history. Columbus's expedition, which was funded by Spain, and his subsequent discovery, spurred other countries to act. Five years after Columbus made his first journey to the Caribbean Islands,

This portrait of Jacques Cartier (1491–1557) was completed in 1545. On his first voyage in 1534, he crossed the Atlantic Ocean in twenty days and landed on an island near Newfoundland. He then sailed north where, on two separate occasions, he met the Micmac and Huron Indians. Cartier took the Huron chief's sons to France to become interpreters. It was on his second voyage, when he was able to further explore the St. Lawrence River, that he realized that a Northwest Passage to Asia was not possible.

another Italian navigator, Giovanni Caboto, landed somewhere along the coast of Labrador or Newfoundland. Caboto claimed the land for Great Britain, which had financed Caboto's exploration. To the British settlers who sailed to North America later, Caboto was known as John Cabot.

Initially, however, it was not land that tempted Europeans to explore Canada further. Word quickly spread throughout Europe that the seas off the coast of northeast Canada were teeming with fish, and the waters were soon filled with fishing boats from a variety of European countries.

A Quest for Natural Resources

Great Britain had made the first European claim to the lands of Canada's east coast, but it was the French who financed and led the first explorations into the North American

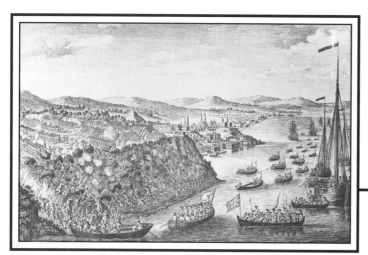

In 1759, during the Seven Years' War, General James Wolfe commanded the largest British naval force to ever cross the Atlantic. The fleet consisted of one-fourth of the entire Royal Navy, two hundred transports, storage vessels, provision ships, and nearly 9,000 soldiers. They landed off the Island of Orleans in the St. Lawrence River with the intent to capture Québec.

This map of Hochelaga (present-day Montréal) in New France was the first printed map of a settlement in North America, published between 1556 and 1606. Cartier visited this Iroquois settlement in 1535 and described it in the account of his second trip to Canada. When he arrived at Hochelaga, he found nearly 2,000 Iroquois Indians living there in a village that he renamed Mount Royal. The rapids to the north and south of Montréal Island prevented Cartier from continuing his expeditions westward in search of a Northwest Passage.

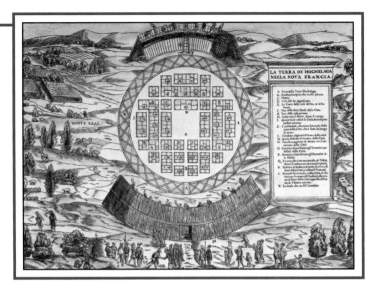

interior. In the mid-1500s, a French mariner named Jacques Cartier made three voyages to North America. While exploring the Gulf of St. Lawrence in search of a passageway to Asia, Cartier first heard the word "kanata." Two Iroquois guides who accompanied the Cartier expedition made repeated references to "kanata," an Iroquoian word that meant

An eyewitness of the capture of Québec on September 13, 1759, drew this illustration. The British made many unsuccessful attempts to seize Québec because of its natural fortification, it being situated on a high plateau and surrounded by steep, rocky cliffs and the St. Lawrence River. However, when the British finally got their chance on the night of September 12, British troops used a lightly guarded passageway to gain access through the cliffs to the Plains of Abraham. Because of the sheer number of the British troops, the French offered little resistance.

Jacques Cartier can be seen in this lithograph speaking with Canadian Indians in the village of Hochelaga, on the present-day site of Montréal. Soon after the meeting, Cartier reportedly climbed nearby Mount Royal to survey the region and saw for the first time the Lachine Rapids and the Ottawa River. It was the explorer's second voyage (1535–1536) to Canada for France under the command of King Francis I.

village or settlement. Cartier misinterpreted what the guides were saying, and in his diaries made reference to "kanata." Among Europeans, the word would soon became synonymous with Canada, the land Cartier would claim for France.

Though interest in finding a passageway to the west ebbed, the desire to develop Canada as a source of natural resources remained strong. However, attempts to establish permanent settlements there were met with failure. The climate was often harsh and the native peoples, though frequently helpful, were not tolerant of the Europeans' attempts to settle the land permanently.

More than any natural resource, it was the abundance of fur that, despite setbacks, fueled France's interest in settling the region. The fur trade was not only responsible for the exploration of Canada but also France's decision to establish New France, a French colonial outpost located in present-day Québec. Still, by 1625, only about fifty Frenchmen lived there permanently.

Great Britain disputed France's Canadian land claims. The British, who had established settlements south of Québec as well as along the coast, often clashed with the French. The Seven Years' War, fought between the French and British between 1756 and 1763, was one such conflict. Great Britain was victorious and established its authority in Québec, ruling the formerly French territory. According to British law, Catholics were denied the right to vote or to hold public office. This was an unpopular policy among the French, nearly all of whom were Catholic. In 1774, in an effort to gain the loyalty of its new French subjects, the British Parliament passed the Québec Act, which recognized the civil and religious rights of the French. It was a decision that would mark the beginning of political and cultural conflicts between the French and English within Canada.

This painting depicts the Fathers of Confederation ending their daily tasks as John A. Macdonald rises to speak. These representatives of the British North American colonies attended one or more of three major conferences—the Charlottetown Conference in 1864, the Québec Conference in 1864, and the London Conference in 1866. These conferences led to the unification of Canada in 1867. Led by John A. Macdonald, the Fathers sought to unify the provinces of Canada under one Canadian federal government overseen by England's Crown. This legislation, passed on July 1, 1867, became known as the British North America Act and remained enforced until 1982 when Canada became independent.

Canada's population grew quickly in the early 1800s, as thousands of immigrants from England, Ireland, and Scotland flooded its shores. By the mid-1800s, its population numbered almost 2.5 million. Britain had divided the country into two colonies, Upper Canada and Lower Canada, and most of the new immigrants settled in Upper Canada. French Canadians, who dominated Lower Canada, were angered by the influx of British immigrants, and several revolts broke out. In 1841, in an effort to unite the country, the British Parliament passed the Act of Union, which united the two Canadian colonies into the Province of Canada. In 1867, the British North America Act joined the provinces of Canada, Prince Edward Island, Nova Scotia, and New Brunswick into one country.

As the numbers of European immigrants in Canada grew, the indigenous population shrunk. Not only did their numbers suffer as a result of conflict, their population was decimated by European diseases to which they had no natural immunity. In addition to smallpox and measles, the English and French also brought with them alcohol. Large numbers of the native population soon fell victim to alcoholism and its attendant problems, including unemployment, poverty, and poor health.

Colonization of the West

While Canada's population grew steadily throughout the late 1800s, its neighbor to the south, the United States, grew at an even more dramatic rate. During this time, the United States experienced a population boom, due in large part to industrialization and poor conditions in Europe. The United States quickly expanded west, as new immigrants and longtime residents sought opportunity on the frontier. Fear of the United States's growing power led to the creation of the Confederation of Canada. Approved by the British Parliament in 1867, the British North American Act granted Canada the right to self-government. As part of the agreement, Britain continued to handle the colony's foreign affairs, and the British monarch served as the head of state.

Concerned that the United States's aggressive expansion might eventually encroach upon Canadian territory, the Canadian government also began a massive publicity

Crowds in this busy Vancouver port *(above right)* welcome the arrival of the first train to the city from the East in May 1887. Official construction of the Canadian Pacific Railway (CPR) began in 1881 in order to unite the Canadian coasts. The CPR received $25 million and 25 million acres of land in exchange for building the railway through rugged terrain. The CPR then sold the underdeveloped land to settlers to colonize the western area until they reached the less hospitable lands of Saskatchewan and Alberta. Donald A. Smith *(below right)* financed much of the CPR's construction and was given the honor of driving the last spike at Craigellachie, British Columbia, on November 7, 1885.

Sir Wilfred Laurier (1841–1919) was the first French Canadian prime minister. Laurier is considered one of the greatest leaders in Canadian history. His ideals of a national identity for Canada were popular among both Conservative and Liberal parties, though his administration was not well received by the British. Along with unifying the country, Laurier created the Yukon Territory and Saskatchewan and Alberta provinces, settled the Alaska boundary dispute, and constructed the second transcontinental railway.

campaign, promising free land to immigrants willing to make a new start in the country's western territories. The new immigrants, generally of European descent, were taken westward on trains along the newly completed Canadian Pacific transcontinental railroad.

Though many frontier settlers returned home, beaten by the rugged lifestyle, thousands remained. The perseverance and bravery of these early settlers led to the formation, in 1905, of the new provinces of Saskatchewan and Alberta. The addition of the two western provinces established Canada's coast-to-coast dominance, which was made complete when Newfoundland joined the Canadian Confederation in 1949.

Postwar Changes and Challenges

Canada prospered during the first part of the twentieth century, but like the rest of the world, it

This Canadian poster rallies support for overseas troops during World War II (1939–1945). Canadian forces joined British forces during the early years of the war and were instrumental in freeing Italy from fascist control, helping to initiate the surrender of Germany at the Battle of Hochwald Ridge. Canadian forces also supported the British air force and navy with pilots, navigators, aerial gunners, and bombardiers. Prime Minister Mackenzie King promised that a draft for overseas service would not be enacted; however, as the war wore on, the draft became necessary. Draftees were sent to Europe in 1944 following the Normandy invasion.

The People: The Ancient First Nations and the Modern Canadians

Canada's twelfth prime minister, Louis Saint Laurent (1882–1973), who served from 1948 to 1957, is pictured in this photograph. Laurent encouraged the industrial boom that began in Canada after World War II. Government programs were created to enable veterans to buy homes and businesses and receive loans for the purposes of education. The discovery of new oil and iron-ore reserves also led to an increase in manufacturing and the development of improved infrastructure.

struggled during the Great Depression and World War II. As Canada began to rebuild its economy in the 1940s, the focus of its citizens shifted from international to domestic issues. As in the past, French Canadians expressed frustration with the government's failure to recognize and celebrate their culture.

From 1968 until 1984, when talk of secession was common among French Canadians in Québec, Prime Minister Pierre Elliott Trudeau, a French Canadian and an extremely popular leader across ethnic divides, worked to maintain a united Canada. Trudeau promised to create a nation that was more culturally and politically inclusive of French Canadians. In 1969, he won Parliament's approval of the Official Languages Act, which required federal facilities to provide services in French, as well as English, in areas where at least 10 percent of the population spoke French.

Trudeau is also well known as the prime minister who, with the Constitution Act of 1982, ended Britain's authority to veto amendments to Canada's constitution. Today, the people of Canada are politically independent from Great Britain and the British Parliament.

This photograph of Canadian troops and German prisoners resting in a trench at Canal du Nord in France was taken in September 1918 at the Battle of Arras, a major conflict on the Western Front during World War I (1914–1918). The Eighth Canadian Brigade led the attack, pushing back the Germans and reaching the occupied trench of Canal du Nord.

Queen Elizabeth II and Canadian prime minister Pierre Trudeau are pictured signing the Canadian constitution on April 17, 1982. The constitution gave Canada full legal independence from Great Britain and included a Charter of Rights and Freedoms for all Canadians. An independent Canadian government was the dream of Trudeau, who served Canada for sixteen years and saw to the birth of Canada's independence, its Official Languages Act, and public support for the unity of the nation and against the separation of Québec.

French Canadians were not alone in their fight for greater recognition and expanded civil rights. During the 1960s, a number of minority groups emerged with similar concerns. In 1970, two new native groups, the Canadian Métis Society and the National Indian Brotherhood, were organized to promote unity among indigenous people. As the civil rights movement took center stage in the United States, African Americans in Canada also rallied for better treatment by the government.

The New Faces of Immigration

During the 1970s, the Canadian population changed in two ways. The population was growing older as the young adults of Canada went elsewhere for education and work. In addition, there was an increasing number of immigrants arriving in Canada from countries in Africa, Asia, and South America. In 1976, 1978, and 1987, immigration legislation was reformed to encourage immigration from nontraditional sources.

The People: The Ancient First Nations and the Modern Canadians

An Inuit family poses on Baffin Island. The Canadian government mandated that the Indian and Inuit people have the right of self-government, a decision that came after land disputes between indigenous Canadians and the government. A major victory for the Inuit occurred in 1992 when voters in the Northwest Territories authorized the division of their land into two separate territories, one of which would become a self-governing Inuit homeland called Nunavut.

During the 1990s, political and social upheaval in Sri Lanka, Taiwan, and Hong Kong spurred emigration from those countries to Canada. By the turn of the twenty-first century, almost 5 million residents, or about 16 percent of Canada's total population, were born abroad. Most of these new immigrants flocked to Canada's cities. Their large numbers, combined with their perhaps unfamiliar appearance, cultures, and languages, caused some Canadians to respond to this new wave of immigrants with resentment and, in some cases, violence.

Overall, however, Canadians have always prided themselves on their openness to other cultures. In response to the new wave of immigrants, the government began funding services and publications devoted to assisting newcomers to Canada, the numbers of which grow steadily each year.

In the late 1990s, the Canadian government also made an effort to correct the many years of unequal treatment experienced by its indigenous people. In 1999, the government announced the establishment of a new territory called Nunavut. Carved out of the eastern Northwest Territories, Nunavut was created to provide more self-government for the Inuit, who make up most of its population.

Canada, like those who settled and persevered in this often challenging land, has evolved into a country that has not only endured but prospered. As a result, Canada is recognized as a world power whose greatest strength is its desire to respect the contributions of its entire population.

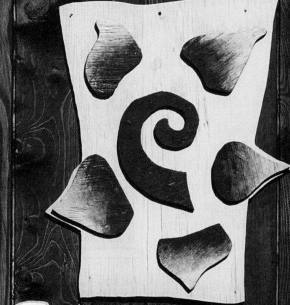

THE LANGUAGES OF CANADA

3

From Indigenous Tongues to Modern English

Since 1969, Canada has had two official languages, English and French. However, the controversy over which language Canadians should speak dates back to before the country was formed. Since England and France's near simultaneous arrival in Canada, there have been innumerable battles over political and cultural supremacy. Many of the lines that have been drawn between those two cultures are based on language. In England's and France's efforts to dominate the culture linguistically, little attention was paid to respecting, much less maintaining, the languages of the First Nations.

At the start of the new century, battles are still being fought over language. Many French Canadians remain resentful of the dominance of English culture. Since the 1970s, indigenous Canadians have asserted their right to speak their languages, as well as teach them to their children. Immigrants who speak neither French nor English have also created new controversies.

The Languages of the First Nations

Canada's indigenous population is estimated to have occupied the land for approximately 15,000 years before Europeans arrived. Without any written records, anthropologists have used language as one method to differentiate the various indigenous groups. The subarctic peoples belong to two regionally based language groups. The

This photograph of a French sign *(left)* was taken in the city of Québec. Canada is officially bilingual, and all services provided by the federal government are in French and English. There are also a few unofficial languages spoken in Canada, such as Chinese, Italian, Punjabi, Spanish, Portuguese, and Polish. This photograph *(above)* shows a couple shopping in downtown Montréal. In the dominantly French-speaking cities such as this one, there are an increasing number of mixed marriages between English- and French-speaking Canadians, who raise bilingual children.

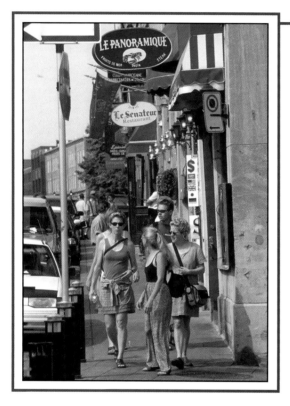

The women in this photograph are shopping in the French city of Montréal. In Canada, each province has the ability to declare its common language. Nine provinces have declared English as the common language while recognizing French second. French is the common language in Québec.

Algonquin-speaking people were located in regions that ranged from northwest of the Great Lakes to the upper shields of Québec and Labrador. More than twenty Athabascan languages were spoken among the people of the western subarctic; they are known today as the Dene.

Despite efforts by the French and British colonial governments to blot out native tongues, about fifty indigenous languages have endured. The first French and English settlers adopted words from the languages of the First Nations that are still part of the French and English languages today. Significantly, many of Canada's well-known cities and landmarks have names with indigenous origins. The name Canada is based on an Iroquois word that means village or settlement. Today many members of Canada's First Nations speak their own languages.

A Battle for Survival and Supremacy

Since the arrival of the first Europeans in Canada, the battle for cultural dominance between the French and the British has continued. Over time, this conflict has itself become a part of Canada's identity. Though Great Britain was the first nation to plant a flag on Canadian soil, the French were the first successful explorers of Canada's interior and its first settlers.

Following the Seven Years' War (1756–1763), the British gained control of Canada and initially attempted to diminish the power of its French citizens through a series of laws that denied Catholics the right to vote, be elected, or hold public office.

Had Britain not had to contend with both its geographical distance from Canada, the continued battles with native peoples, and efforts by the thirteen colonies to throw

This man browses through magazines at a retail shop. There are an estimated ninety languages in Canada. After French and English, Chinese is the most widely used first language. There are also a number of indigenous languages spoken, such as Cree and Inuktitut.

off English rule, history might have been different. As it happened, the English were in desperate need of their French citizens' loyalty. As a result, the British Parliament passed the Québec Act in 1774, which helped preserve the French language.

Differences Along Language Lines

In the early 1800s, the country was flooded by English-speaking immigrants from England, Ireland, and Scotland. At the time, Canada was politically divided into Upper and Lower Canada. The French, who largely lived in Upper Canada, resented this influx of English-speaking immigrants. Many were convinced that the wave of immigration was part of the British government's plan to destroy French heritage in Canada. Many French Canadians rebelled, and in response, the British government joined Upper Canada and Lower Canada. In addition, the British Parliament granted the united colony greater power to self-govern.

As Canada expanded westward and its English-speaking population grew, Québec became a stronghold for French-speaking Canadians. In addition to domestic issues, debates about Canada's international policies were often drawn along language lines. One such debate occurred in 1910. Britain faced the threat of war with Germany, and so Parliament asked Canada to supply ships and sailors. English-speaking Canadians were in favor of supporting the British war effort, but French-speaking Canadians were opposed to the idea, charging that it would involve Canada in a dangerous foreign war.

A Threat to Unity

In the 1960s, disagreements related to differences in language threatened to tear the country apart. In 1960, the provincial government of Québec initiated the Quiet Revolution, which was a movement to defend French Canadian rights throughout

License plates in Québec are inscribed with the province's motto "Je me souviens," or "I remember." This motto has appeared on license plates in Québec since 1978, but the words themselves date back to 1883 when the Québec government ratified the proposal of architect Eugène-Étienne Taché to place the province's coat of arms above the door of the parliament building with this motto.

the country. Many French Canadians felt they were discriminated against because they spoke French. They also wanted to protect their heritage in a country that was dominated by English speakers.

Inspired by the Quiet Revolution, some French-speaking Canadians began to discuss becoming an independent nation. One group, the Front de Libération du Québec (FLQ), used terrorism to promote its vision of separatism.

Shortly after Pierre Trudeau, Canada's third prime minister, came into office, he went to work on uniting French- and English-speaking Canada. Trudeau was born in Montréal on October 18, 1919. His father was a French Canadian, and his mother was a Canadian of Scottish descent. He grew up in a bilingual and bicultural household, which may have contributed to his strong belief that French and English Canada should stay united. His popularity with all Canadians enabled him to help pass the Official Languages Act in 1969. The act required government facilities to provide services in French in areas where at least 10 percent of the population speaks French.

The signage on this ice-cream shop in Old Montréal appears in French, the official language of the city. Language laws require that French text in commercial signage be twice as large as the English translation when it appears with English. A news story focusing on this controversy cited a case where a business was fined for a handwritten sign in English that read "push" that was attached to a washroom door.

French and English newspapers are printed throughout Canada. Many of the major cities, whether officially French- or English-speaking, have newspapers printed in both languages.

The law did little to quell the separatist movement. Eleven years later, in 1980, a vote was held in Québec that would have given the provincial government the right to negotiate with the federal government for independence. Approximately 60 percent of Québec's voters rejected the proposal. There was yet another separatist vote in 1994, and once again, the referendum for Québec's independence was defeated.

A Diversity of Languages

French and English are the official languages of Canada, and the 1996 Canadian census revealed that 19 million Canadians, or 60 percent of the population, spoke English, and 6.5 million Canadians, or 22.5 percent, spoke French. Though the number of people speaking English has not changed since the 1970s, the number of French speakers has declined by about 3 percent. Close to 20 percent of Canadians are bilingual, a ratio that has increased.

After English and French, the most common language spoken in Canada is Chinese. The Chinese are part of a new wave of non-European immigrants who entered the country after Canada removed discriminatory sections from its immigration law in the 1960s. In 1996, more than 225,000 immigrants entered Canada.

Canada's long history of contending with the often unhappy marriage of two distinct cultures and languages has benefited those immigrants who speak neither French nor English. Programs vary from province to province, but in general, Canada has displayed a high level of commitment to multiculturalism. More than five hundred years after the British and French explorers first set foot in Canada, division along language lines remains a defining force, though the country remains intact as a nation.

CANADIAN MYTHS AND LEGENDS

4

Myths, legends, and folklore are abundant in Canada. These tales are rooted in the storytelling traditions of Canada's indigenous and early European settlers, who, finding themselves in a vast and often intimidating landscape, told stories as both a form of entertainment and as a way to understand or feel less intimidated by their new environment.

A myth is a traditional story that deals with ancestors, supernatural beings, or heroes. It appeals to the people who share it because it gives expression to deep, commonly held emotions and beliefs. What one culture labels as myth, another culture might know as expressions of a religious belief. A legend is an unverified, popular story handed down from one generation to the next. Often a legend is loosely based on a historic event. Legends were widely used by preliterate societies, meaning those societies that did not have a written alphabet. This explains why so many of Canada's best-loved myths and legends were first told by Canada's native population, a group of people that did not have a written language. There are also modern-day legends, which are often referred to as urban legends.

Lacking a written tradition, the myths and legends told by Canada's indigenous population served a variety of

This memorial pole *(left)* carved by Willie Seaweed depicts a thunderbird and a Dzunukwa, a mythological female often referred to as the wild woman of the woods. Memorial poles were erected by the chief of an Indian tribe's heir as part of the process of assuming his predecessor's rights and privileges. Seaweed was the son of a Kwakiutl Indian chief and renowned Canadian artist who used animals and creatures from his peoples' legends in his works. This Inuit mask *(above)* depicts a raven and was likely made of spruce or cottonwood and carved with metal tools.

The Inuit mask seen in this photograph depicts a red bear. In the Inuit culture, masks are largely used for dancing in religious ceremonies or festivals. Inuit dances have various cultural meanings that illustrate the human condition and experience. Every mask the dancer wears has its own story to represent its specific meaning—most often a visionary statement of its creator.

important purposes. In addition to serving as a basis for their spiritual belief system, they also held a range of lessons on topics ranging from how one is expected to behave socially to the traditional wisdom pertaining to hunting and gathering food.

Indigenous Myths and Legends

Many native Canadian myths were centered on critical life passages. The Ojibway, who had some connections with the Algonquin and whose original homeland stretched from central Saskatchewan to southern Ontario, told a story that explained why humans were mortal. In addition to being an enjoyable tale, this story is rich with historic information, including where the Ojibway lived and how they envisioned the afterlife.

The story centers around the figure of Nanabush, a great Ojibway hero, who was responsible for creating the world. Nanabush was called on by the Creator to walk east until he reached a swift-running river, which he was to walk across without a moment's hesitation. The river was both fast and deep and made even more treacherous by rocks. When he reached the river, Nanabush hesitated for just a moment before crossing. There was a beautiful woman waiting on the other side of the bank, and when he reached her, she explained that she was his wife, sent to him by the Creator.

Nanabush and his wife settled near a river, built a home, and raised many children. These children were the first of the Ojibway people. Unlike their father, who was immortal, the children grew older with each day. They were the first humans.

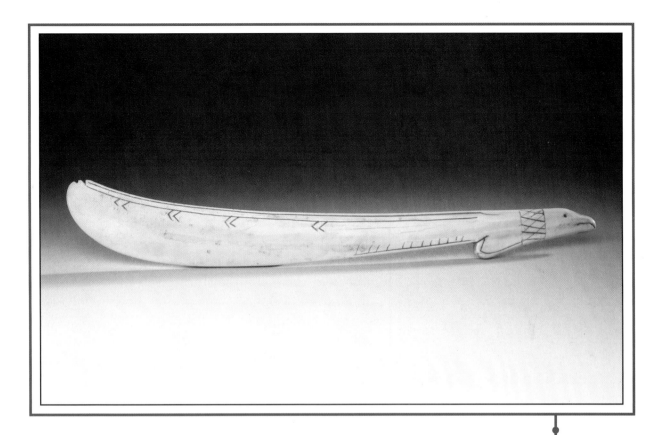

They could not live forever because, so many years before, Nanabush had doubted the Creator and hesitated for just a moment before crossing the river. Eventually, they were taken away to the land of spirits.

Another story told by the Ojibway explains how butterflies were created. The story says that long ago, human twins were born to the spirit woman. The spirit woman relied on animals to take care of her two children. The animals spoiled the children, who had no reason to walk or even stand. They were completely looked after. The animals called on Nanabush to help the children, and he in turn asked the spirit woman for advice. She instructed him to search along the slope of a mountain, where he would find thousands of brightly colored stones. Nanabush did as he was told. He gathered the stones and began to toss handfuls of them toward the sky. The stones, however, did not fall back down to the ground. Instead they turned into a flock of brightly colored butterflies. They followed Nanabush back to the lazy twins, who were immediately inspired to reach out their arms to catch the beautiful creatures. Soon the

Pictured in this photograph is an Inuit storytelling knife. The Inuit use a decorated knife to draw pictures in the snow or mud as a way of enhancing the oral tradition of storytelling. The Inuit culture is highly visual and aware of the landscape and surrounding nature as they work the land and hunt. Largely reflected in their history, the Inuit use storytelling as a way of retaining their language and myths. Since they had no written language, they are a people who relied heavily on oral tradition.

This Ojibway rock painting, located on the shore of Lake Superior, Ontario, depicts Missipeshu, an imaginary spirit animal that is half lynx and half serpent. It is believed that an Ojibway tribal shaman painted it to represent the danger of turbulent water. In 1850, the Ojibway Midewiwin Society claimed that this pictograph is part of a larger work that tells the story of a heroic crossing of Lake Superior.

twins were crawling, then walking, and even running in an effort to catch the butterflies.

These myths tell a lot about the native people who told them. Animals are given the roles of the children's caretakers, suggesting how highly they were regarded. We also learn that the people who enjoyed this story lived in a mountainous region. In addition, we discover that while life may have been hard and survival precarious, it is clear from the story that the Ojibway still had time to take pleasure in nature's beauty.

There is also a strong French narrative tradition in Canada. Heroes that repeatedly appear in these French myths and legends include a great hero called Ti-Jean, a fearless hunter named Dalbec, and Jean Cadieux, a voyager whose tragic death is remembered in a French Canadian folk song.

Modern Legends

Though the practice of telling stories may be less common than it was long ago, legends and myths are still very much a part of Canadian society. Myths and legends about modern society are passed along in much the same way as traditional ones once were. The only difference is the added impact of modern forms of communication such as the telephone and the Internet.

The media has been known to create or perpetuate news items that are actually nothing more than the product of someone's very active imagination. One such urban legend claims that White River, Ontario, is the coldest place in Canada. That superlative, in fact, belongs to Iroquois Falls, in eastern Canada, where the temperature was recorded at -72 degrees Fahrenheit (-58.3° Celsius) in January 1935. Like most legends, the White River legend has some basis in fact. In the early days of radio, White River was one of only a handful of cities that transmitted its weather conditions on a daily basis. As a result, when news stations announced the coldest daily temperature in the nation, it was often that of White River. Newscasters failed to mention, however, that their data was limited.

Canadian E-mail Charge

The following is a modern urban legend that was circulated on the Internet. There is no Bill 602P and the Canadian Post has not tried to charge Canadians for e-mail. However, many Canadians who received this e-mail believed it was true and, in turn, e-mailed it to other Canadians.

Please read the following carefully if you intend to stay on-line and continue using e-mail:

Under proposed legislation Canada Post will be attempting to bill e-mail users out of "alternate postage fees." Bill 602P will permit the federal government to charge a 5-cent surcharge on every e-mail delivered, by billing Internet Service Providers at source. The consumer would then be billed in turn by the ISP.

The Canada Post Corporation is claiming that lost revenue due to the proliferation of e-mail is costing nearly $23,000,000 in revenue per year. Since the average citizen received about 10 e-mails per day, the cost to the typical individual would be an additional 50 cents per day, or over $180 dollars per year. Note that this would be money paid directly to Canada Post for a service they do not even provide.

The whole point of the Internet is democracy and non-interference. If the Canadian government is permitted to tamper with our liberties by adding a surcharge to e-mail, who knows where it will end. You are already paying an exorbitant price for snail mail because of beaurocratic inefficiency.

It currently takes up to 6 days for a letter to be delivered from Mississauga to Scarborough. If Canada Post Corporation is allowed to tinker with e-mail, it will mark the end of the free Internet in Canada. Note that most of the major newspapers have ignored the story, the only exception being the *Toronto Star*, which called the idea of e-mail surcharge "a useful concept who's time has come." Don't sit by and watch your freedoms erode away! Send this e-mail to all Canadians on your list and tell your friends and relatives to write their representatives and say "No!" to Bill 602P.

This photograph of a Haida Indian village was taken in 1900. The Haida lived on Haida Gwaii, a cluster of islands off the northern coast of British Columbia, and was once the most powerful of Canada's indigenous tribes. The Haida had two *moieties*, or tribal subdivisions, the raven and the eagle. The raven was divided into twenty-two lineages or families, while the eagle had twenty-three. Marriage was not permitted between people of the same moiety, and children became part of their mother's lineage. Each lineage gave its members certain resources such as hunting and fishing grounds, collecting areas, house sites, and rights to certain myths, dances, legends, and songs.

In recent years, the Internet has proven to be a fertile breeding ground for the perpetuation of urban legends. Though the stories are written rather than spoken, the simple click of a mouse can relay information to countless viewers. In addition, information is rarely checked for accuracy, and the anonymity of the Web makes it difficult to refer to a source. The Internet has been home to both the revival of some long-dead legends, as well as the start of several new tall tales.

Preserving Canada's Tradition

Canada's myths and legends are not simply a collection of outdated stories. They are an important part of the country's history. By studying the myths and legends of

Canada's indigenous population, we can learn about their religious beliefs and culture and how they survived from day to day. The same can be said of French and British myths and legends.

These stories, along with other forms of traditional verbal expression, including folk songs, drama, riddles, proverbs, and sayings, are all forms of Canadian folklore. There is also nonverbal folklore, such as arts and crafts, dance, and music.

In an effort to learn from and preserve Canadian folklore, it has been researched and recorded in a variety of forms. There are many books on folklore, and it is the focus of extensive research at several prominent Canadian universities. In addition to efforts to study and record Canadian folklore, there has been a movement among Canada's native population to uncover their cultural roots, including the ancient tradition of storytelling. For many people in the country's indigenous population, a revival of the traditional practice of storytelling is a way to restore some of what was taken from their ancestors during European colonization. The Europeans often not only banned the use of indigenous languages in school but also made every effort to supplant the native peoples' religions with Christianity. For the vast majority of Canada's history, information was passed orally from person to person. As such, the myths and legends that have survived today are connections to Canada's past indigenous ancestors.

CANADIAN FESTIVALS AND CEREMONIES OF ANTIQUITY AND TODAY

5

The Canadian government recognizes ten official holidays that, for the most part, celebrate the country's British and Christian heritage. Many holidays are officially celebrated on a Friday or Monday that falls near the original date of the holiday. This provides federal employees and other workers with three-day weekends.

Regional differences are highlighted by holidays celebrated by some provinces but not others. For example, only Québec celebrates St. Jean Baptiste Day, which is observed on June 24. There are also seasonal celebrations, musical gatherings, and parades with a variety of cultural themes that represent the country's mixed culture and interests.

Canada's ten official holidays represent a mix of seasonal celebrations, patriotic observations, and religious events. On these days, the federal government is closed, as are the country's banks and many businesses. The ten federal holidays are New Year's Day, Good Friday, Easter Monday, Victoria Day, Canada Day, Labor Day, Thanksgiving Day, Remembrance Day, Christmas Day, and Boxing Day.

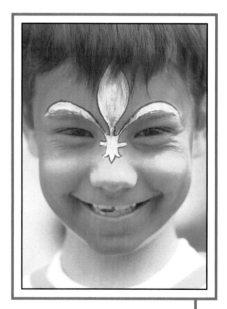

The couple in this photograph *(left)*, dressed in British Columbia and Canada flags, hand out souvenir flags as part of the Canada Day celebrations. Canada Day, celebrated on July 1, commemorates the British North America Act of 1867, which created the Canadian federal government. Before 1982, however, when Canada was politically tied to England, this day was known as Dominion Day, proclaimed by the British North America Act as a country "one Dominion under the name of Canada." The child with face paint *(above)* celebrates St. Jean Baptiste Day to honor the patron saint of the French Canadians.

This yard in Québec is decorated for Halloween, which is celebrated in much the same fashion as it is in the United States. The Canadian Halloween tradition began with the arrival of British immigrants in the 1800s who had been celebrating a form of Halloween in Europe for years. Trick-or-treating and carving jack-o-lanterns in pumpkins instead of the Irish tradition of using turnips is commonplace.

New Year's Day

January 1, New Year's Day, is the date of the official federal holiday, but most Canadians celebrate the beginning of the new year the night before. New Year's Eve parties often begin in the evening and are attended by family and friends. Canadians often make New Year's resolutions, which are goals for making positive changes in one's personal or professional life over the course of the coming year.

Good Friday and Easter

The dates for both Good Friday and Easter Sunday vary from year to year because they fall on the weekend after the first full moon after the March 21 spring equinox. Religious historians have pointed out that Easter's connection with the equinox reflects the pagan roots of this Christian holiday.

Good Friday is the most solemn day in the Christian calendar. It commemorates the crucifixion of Jesus Christ. Easter, which celebrates the resurrection of Jesus Christ, falls on the Sunday following Good Friday. Easter's pagan roots are

expressed in the tradition of the Easter rabbit, a magical creature who brings goodies to children on Easter morning. The rabbit and the eggs he often bears are symbols of the Norse goddess Ostar and represent fertility.

Labor Day

Held on the first Monday in September, this holiday has lost much of its meaning as a day to honor laborers. For most Canadians, Labor Day simply signals the end of summer, when vacationers return home and children prepare to go back to school. It is summer's final celebration, and many people make travel plans in an effort to get in one last weekend of rest and relaxation before the cold weather of fall and winter begins.

Christmas in Canada is celebrated much like it is in the United States, though it is influenced by French and British traditions. In Nova Scotia, for example, songs and carols brought from Britain two centuries ago are sung each Christmas morning. During the twelve days of Christmas, small groups appear in neighborhoods often making noise and seeking candy or other treats.

Thanksgiving Day

Thanksgiving is a national secular holiday that was introduced to Canada by American immigrants in the eighteenth century. In Canada, Thanksgiving is celebrated on the

This is a photograph of the Calgary Stampede and Exhibition celebrated in Calgary, Alberta, for ten days every July. Millions of people from around the world travel to Calgary each year to take part in this festival, a popular tourist attraction that began in 1886. Some people think that it is reminiscent of the Old West with events such as rodeos, amusements, concerts, and chuck-wagon races.

second Monday in October, while in the United States it is celebrated on the fourth Thursday in November. This difference reflects Canada's shorter harvest season, a consequence of its geography. For Canadian Thanksgiving, family and friends gather to give thanks for a bountiful harvest and enjoy a large afternoon meal.

Christmas and Boxing Day

Christmas is a Christian holiday that celebrates the birth of Jesus Christ and falls on December 25. Almost all businesses close on that day, and people who celebrate the holiday often attend church services in the morning and gather with friends and family for a large meal. Children often receive many gifts. This tradition reflects the story of Santa Claus, who lives at the North Pole where he and his elves make toys for well-behaved children from all over the world.

The day after Christmas, December 26, is known as Boxing Day. Boxing Day originated in Great Britain in the middle of the nineteenth century. The day was

This Canadian military veteran, who fought with the Royal Canadian Engineers during World War II and in the Korean War, wears his old uniform as he marches in a Remembrance Day parade. Remembrance Day is held annually on November 11 since it originally commemorated the day World War I ended. Many people wear poppies as a reminder of the people who were killed in the fields where they grow in Flanders, France, where much of the fighting during World War I occurred.

traditionally celebrated by servants and tradespeople, who often had to work during Christmas. In Canada, it is simply a day spent with family and friends. More gifts are exchanged, and large meals are shared.

Festive Occasions

There are hundreds of major and minor festivals and parades held in Canada each year. Many of these festivals have indigenous roots and mark the arrival of a season or a period following a harvest. There are also festivals that celebrate the heritage and ancestry of a variety of cultures. Following the lead of Canada's indigenous population, many Canadians attend festivals that celebrate the arrival of spring. In April, there are numerous maple syrup festivals held in Nova Scotia and Québec. In Nova Scotia, there is the annual Annapolis Valley Apple Blossom Festival, and in British Columbia, there is an annual Blossom Festival. Canada is proud of its efforts to encourage multiculturalism, and its numerous ethnic festivals attest to this commitment.

The people in this photograph are in Montréal for the annual International Jazz Festival, which is held for two weeks each summer. It began in 1980 with approximately 12,000 music lovers. Today, millions of jazz enthusiasts visit the festival.

THE RELIGIONS OF CANADA THROUGHOUT ITS HISTORY

6

C anada has no official religion, and Canadians are free to practice whatever faith they choose. Echoing the duality of its culture, the vast majority of Canadians are either Roman Catholic or Protestant. Until the mid-nineteenth century, Catholics and Protestants were divided according to nationality. For the most part, the French were Roman Catholic and the British were Protestant. As a greater mix of Europeans immigrated into Canada, these ethnic lines became blurred, though the country remained overwhelmingly Christian until the first half of the twentieth century.

Even today, 80 percent of Canadians define themselves as Christian, while the remaining 20 percent are divided among the world's major religions, including Judaism, Islam, Hinduism, and Sikhism. In addition to the religions practiced by Canada's more recent arrivals, much of the country's indigenous population still holds a wide variety of spiritual beliefs passed down to them by ancestors who occupied Canada long before the arrival of the Europeans.

Reflecting on the Land

The religious practices of the First Nations varied greatly from group to group. In general, their spiritual beliefs reflected their close relationship to and dependence on the land, and these beliefs differed greatly from the institutional religions that came to Canada with the first Europeans.

The Notre Dame Basilica in Montréal *(left)* was constructed between 1825 and 1841 to seat as many as 10,000 worshipers, making it the largest religious building in North America at the time. Designed by James O'Donnell, known for spearheading the neo-Gothic movement, the basilica is classical in structure with a rectangular shape, and gothic in its ornamentation with arched windows and tall towers. This artifact of the Coast Salish tribe *(above)* is worn as a sacred mask to prepare ritual space for the entrance of powerful spirits.

This wooden moon mask from the Kwakuitl tribe is one popular type used among the Kwakuitl people. These masks are made with hinges and strings that when pulled would cause the parts to wiggle, gyrate, or fly apart. These motions create mood and drama for the viewer and can express a variety of emotions.

There is evidence that most indigenous people believed in a supreme creator. However, this belief was not central to their religious practices. Rather, their religions reflected the importance of the things upon which their very lives depended, namely the food they gathered, the animals they hunted, and the climate in which they lived. As such, animals and other products of nature were endowed with spiritual significance, and religious ceremonies occurred according to the changing of the seasons.

The Iroquois, for example, practiced a cycle of thirteen ceremonies of giving thanks. This cycle was related to the agricultural gathering activities of the group. For the native people who settled along the northwest coast, celebration ceremonies were tied to the life cycle of salmon, the fish on which their very survival depended. The people there paid tribute to salmon by acting out stories, and they gave gifts in an effort to ensure the salmon's return in the spring.

Groups that hunted animals often included "dreamers," who received visions from the spirit world that directed them to their quarry. Out of respect for the animal and as a way to give thanks to the spirits, special attention was not only paid to how the animal was caught but also to how it was disposed of and shared.

Lacking a written language, Canada's indigenous people did not have religious books like the Bible, nor were their religious founders of great significance as they were with the world's major religions at the time. Beliefs regarding creation and the connection of people to the spirit world were passed along orally. There were shamans, people whose responsibilities ranged from village doctor to conduit to the spirit world, but generally the spiritual practices of native peoples reflected the society, which was by nature non-hierarchical.

Two Worlds Collide

Beginning in the fifteenth century and continuing on until the eighteenth century, Christianity in Europe was experiencing a period of reform, noteworthy for its high

This sixteenth-century illustration depicts Jacques Cartier conquering New France. When Cartier landed in New France (present-day Canada), he erected the flag of France and a cross to mark the arrival of Christianity. From that time, missionaries were sent to Canada to convert the native peoples. The role of the Catholic Church was important in every aspect of daily life, including its role as an organizer and controller of hospitals.

level of intolerance for any deviation from official belief and practice. The first Europeans in Canada viewed the First Nations as nothing short of savages whose so-called religious practices were clearly pagan in nature. Christian missionaries traveled to Canada with the specific intent of civilizing the indigenous population and converting them to Christianity. In the presence of Europeans, natives followed the teachings of the missionaries, but they practiced their own traditions among their own people.

Despite the attempts by Europeans to permanently squash the religious practices of Canada's indigenous people, their religions are still practiced today. That is not to say

This eighteenth-century engraving shows Europeans and missionaries arriving in Canada. Many French settlements began as Christian mission posts, the largest of which eventually became Montréal. Missionary settlements provided religious instruction and encouraged indigenous people to take active roles in the Christian priesthood.

that Canada's indigenous population has not been influenced by the various European belief systems. Many of Canada's First Nations have converted to Christianity while others observe a combination of belief systems.

The religious beliefs of indigenous Canadians have also been influential. Many of the spirit stories that have been passed down through the ages have become a part of the country's popular culture, and even Canadians without indigenous ancestry celebrate several of the traditional spirit holidays.

The Catholic Church

The first settlers in Canada were French Roman Catholic, though in the beginning years, given the ruggedness of the land, it is likely that the first settlers were more focused on survival than practicing their religion.

After struggling without much success to settle Canada, the French colonial government

This seventeenth-century illustration depicts the baptism of Canada's indigenous population at Port Royal in Nova Scotia. In 1610, through the efforts of Jean de Biencourt, Port Royal was revived as a French settlement and fur trading post. The French were committed to converting the Micmac Indians in the surrounding area to Christianity.

turned to the Catholic Church for assistance. Concerned by the rise of power by Protestant religions at the time, the Catholic Church was eager to provide help. Concerned by the rise in power of Protestant religions during the Protestant Reformation, Catholic leaders were eager to establish their church in new lands. However, in 1620, well over one hundred years after the first settler arrival in Canada, the land was still sparsely colonized. In settlements along the St. Lawrence River, which boasted the largest number of French, just twenty acres had been cultivated, and no more than one hundred French lived there permanently. The church experienced limited success in increasing the Catholic population of Canada. After twenty-five years, the population in nearby Québec had increased to only 1,000. Nonetheless, the spiritual influence of the Catholic Church eventually helped establish a solid foothold of Roman Catholic French in Canada.

Today, in Québec, where Canadian identity remains French, the Roman Catholic Church continues to play a major role in daily life. There are large Catholic populations in other parts of Canada as well, including New Brunswick and Nova Scotia. An influx of Italian and Irish immigrants, who for the most part are Roman Catholic, has meant that Canada's Catholic population is no longer strictly French. Combined, almost half of all Canadians today describe themselves as Roman Catholics.

The Protestant Influence

A series of wars between the British and French colonists ended in 1763, with Britain's conquest of what was then known as New France. In an attempt to weaken the identity of the French, who were, for the most part, members of the Roman Catholic Church, the British government passed a series of laws that denied Catholics the right to vote, to be elected, or to hold public office.

This portrait depicts Joseph Brant (1742–1807), a Mohawk Indian chief whose native name was Thayendanegea. Brant served with the British during the American Revolution and established the first Episcopal church in northern Canada. Brant, who also helped gain Indian support for the British, sided with the Indians because he believed that the colonists, if successful, would take control of Iroquois land. After the Revolutionary War, Brant obtained a land grant in Canada, and he and his people settled in an area of Ontario that would later be named Brantford.

This painting by Canadian artist Paul Kane is titled *North American Medicine Pipe Stem Dance*. Dancing has social and religious functions in many of the native tribes. It serves as a form of prayer, an expression of joy or grief, and a method of becoming one with nature. Like many Native American dances, the medicine dance is based on drumming, which signifies the heartbeat of Mother Nature and also provides its rhythm. Another aspect of Native American dance is the smoking of ceremonial pipes, which are used in a special ritual that involves blowing smoke in each of the four cardinal directions, then skyward, then finally to earth.

The British, the majority of whom identified themselves as Protestant members of the Church of England, were right to fear the power of Catholicism in Canada. At the time of New France's conquest, the Catholic Church held more than one quarter of the land in the colony, and more than one third of the population lived on church-owned estates. Additionally, within Québec, the French population outnumbered the English fifteen to one. French Canadian civilians simply outnumbered the British. In addition, the British faced the threat of revolution in the thirteen colonies along the eastern seaboard of what would one day be called the United States. Across North America, British authority was being questioned and threatened, and assigning second-class status to the French was not a wise move to make.

Britain badly needed the loyalty of its French citizens, and the anti-Catholic laws had the opposite effect. Realizing that the colonies required a different type of rule than the homeland, the British Parliament passed the Québec Act, which recognized the civil and religious rights of French Canadians. In the rebellious thirteen colonies to the south, however, the Québec Act became one of five pieces of legislation grouped under the nickname the Intolerable Acts by the American revolutionaries. During the subsequent American Revolution, the Québec Act curried favor among the members of the Catholic Church, who publicly supported the British cause.

Following the American Revolution, large numbers of Protestant Loyalists relocated to Nova Scotia, Prince Edward Island, and Québec. Loyalists were those who remained loyal to the British Crown throughout the American Revolution. They did not want to assert their independence and form a new country. This influx of Protestant immigrants changed these colonies religiously, politically, and demographically.

In 1867, at the formation of Canada's confederation, 99 percent of its citizens identified themselves as Christian. Roughly 42 percent described themselves as Catholic, and the remaining population was divided among four different Protestant groups—Methodist, Presbyterian, Anglican, and Baptist.

In the one hundred years following confederation, though the country received a large number of immigrants, the religious profile of Canada stayed virtually the same. It was a period marked by relative stability among Canadians. When political battles broke out, however, lines were inevitably drawn along religious or language differences between French-speaking Catholics and English-speaking Protestants.

During the 1960s, religion in Canada changed in two ways. Though there was a steady flow of immigrants into the country, there were proportionately fewer Christians than in the past. Also, among Christian Canadians, church attendance was on the decline, and the number of people claiming no religious affiliation was on the rise.

As of 1999, more than 80 percent of Canadians identified

Biblical figures adorn these stained-glass windows of the Christ Church Cathedral in Montréal, which was completed in 1859. It stands as an important symbol of Montréal's Anglican heritage and was erected for Montréal's then growing Anglican population.

Westminster Abbey in British Columbia, shown in this aerial photograph, is a Benedictine monastery for a group of men who dedicate their lives to God. They follow the teachings of Saint Benedict, who guided monks and nuns in a life of prayer. Westminster Abbey was built in 1954 on a hillside overlooking the Fraser River Valley. Although the monks live a life of solitude, the monastery holds retreats for outsiders who seek solace. One of the most important rules followed by the Benedictine monks is "all guests who come should be welcomed like Christ, for he himself said, 'I was a stranger and you made me welcome.'"

themselves as Christians, with Catholicism being the most dominant sect. The importance of Christianity in Canada is reflected by Christmas, which is the only religious holiday that is also marked as an official federal holiday.

Other Major Religions in Canada

All of the world's major religions have found followers among Canadians. Hinduism, Islam, Judaism, and Sikhism are all practiced by both new immigrants and long-time residents. In the 1991 census, 0.6 percent of Canada's population was Hindu, 0.9 percent Muslim, 1.2 percent Jewish, and 0.5 percent Sikh. Much of Canada's indigenous population declares itself as either Catholic or Protestant, though since the 1960s there has been an emphasis among native people to further embrace the traditional religious practices that abounded before the arrival of the Europeans.

This young Canadian girl is dressed to accept the sacrament of Communion, a rite of passage for young Catholic girls. About 20 percent of Canadians regularly attend church services, compared to 40 percent of Americans.

After World War II, Canada received many Jewish immigrants who were survivors of the Holocaust in Europe. More recently, Jews have immigrated from Eastern Europe and Russia, Israel, South Africa, and the United States. Currently, Canada is home to the fifth largest Jewish community in the world, following the United States, Israel, Russia, and France.

Most members of Canada's Hindu population can trace their roots to Southeast Asia, which includes India, Pakistan, Bangladesh, and Sri Lanka. Southeast Asian immigration to Canada exploded in the 1960s, when racial and national restrictions were removed from Canadian immigration regulations. Most Southeast Asians live in urban environments, especially within Ontario, British Columbia, Alberta, and Québec. In the larger cities within these provinces, Hindu followers have established temples, which are often used by a range of different ethnic groups, in keeping with the principles of the religion.

The 1991 census counted more than 250,000 Muslims, who immigrated to Canada from more than sixty countries. Like most immigrants who came to Canada during or after the 1960s, Muslim immigrants have gravitated to urban regions. Currently, more than 66 percent of the Muslim population lives in Ontario. There are a number of different sects within Islam, and most Canadian Muslims are Sunnis, who, like all Muslims, live according to the guidance of the Koran (Qur'an) and the teachings of Muhammad.

There are more than 15 million practicing Sikhs in the world, and Canada's 2001 census found more than 278,000 living in Canada. Sikhs understand themselves to be part of an ethnicity and a religion. Sikhs worship in *gurdwaras*, or temples, which can be found in all of Canada's major cities. In Ontario alone, there are more than twenty-five gurdwaras. Most Sikhs believe in the importance of prayer, and within a typical

The Religions of Canada Throughout Its History

This reverend speaks at a church in Mansonville, Québec. Canadians have considerable freedom of religion, which is granted by the Charter of Rights and Freedoms. However, the number of Canadians who attend church, mosque, synagogue, or temple is steadily decreasing. Today, only about 30 percent of Canadians feel that religion is personally important.

Sikh family, members rise early so they can read together from the Guru Granth Sahib, which contains Sikh scriptures. With its intense emphasis on community and family life, Sikhism has fared better than many of Canada's other religions, which have lost numbers because of the pressures of assimilation.

In general, however, religion is on the decline in Canada. For example, while 80 percent of Canadians declare themselves Christian, more than 70 percent do not attend any kind of religious service on a regular basis. Additionally, the number of Canadians claiming no religious affiliation is on the rise.

Though the increase in the number of people who claim no affiliation has grown recently, this trend has been linked to the national government's increasing control over social services, which include public health care, counseling, and housing. Religious organizations, no longer needed to provide these services, have diminished in the public's attention. Additionally, while the Christian churches may be losing followers, an increasing number of non-Christians enter the country, and their religious organizations gain relevance by providing the support and community that are essential to the survival of newcomers in any country.

These Sikh men were photographed during prayer in Vancouver. Sikhism is a young religion, but it has risen to the placement of fifth-largest practiced faith in the world with more than 20 million followers. The Indian founder of Sikhism, Guru Nanak, spread a simple message of *ek ong kar*, meaning "we are all one." Nanak's followers became known as Sikhs, or Seekers of the Truth.

69

THE ART AND ARCHITECTURE OF CANADA

7

T oday, the art and architecture of Canada are for the most part influenced by a European aesthetic. The country's best-known artists and architects generally have English or French ancestry. Long before the first Europeans arrived, however, the country's indigenous population was making art and constructing buildings, and their contributions as well as their influence on the Europeans who settled there is part of what makes Canada's art and architecture uniquely Canadian.

Ancient Art

The cultural history of Canada's First Nations dates to the arrival of the first North American explorers approximately fifteen thousand years ago. The art of Canada's indigenous population is divided into three periods: prehistoric art, contact art, and contemporary native art. Unfortunately, because much of the art created by the First Nations was made with perishable materials, little of it survives today.

One well-known form of First Nation art is the totem pole, which was largely a product of indigenous Canadians living on the northwest coast. Intricately carved and painted, the poles often included family crests and representations of animals native to Canada. Though totem poles were carved during the prehistoric period, most of the remaining well-known poles were carved after 1860, during the contact period of First Nation art.

Robson Square *(left)*, a civic center in Vancouver, was designed by Canadian architect Arthur Erickson. The complex contains law courts, the Vancouver Art Gallery, government offices, and a media center. The Inuit hunter in this photograph *(above)* pulls aside the snow brick over the door to his igloo. Once built, the Inuit heat the interior snow blocks until they melt slightly and then allow them to refreeze, making the structure stronger.

These totem poles, carved by the Northwest Indians, are located in Stanley Park in Vancouver. The term "totem pole" refers to the tall cedar poles carved with multiple figures by native people of the Northwest coast. The totem figures are inherited crests that identify the pole owner and the family history. Many tribes stopped carving these monuments in the late 1800s when the *potlatch*, the ceremony held when poles were raised, was made illegal in Canada. In 1951, the Canadian government revoked the anti-potlatch law, and today, native people throughout the Northwest raise new poles to celebrate their heritage.

The contact period gets its name from the first interactions between Canada's indigenous peoples and the European explorers. The arrival of a foreign and unfamiliar culture influenced the art of the First Nations in a variety of ways. The Europeans introduced new materials, such as glass beads, and new technologies, such as the rifle. These innovations changed both the look and subjects of First Nation art. Art made by the First Nations during the contact period is better known than earlier artistic efforts because it was observed and often depicted in the diaries of European explorers.

Native art is widely varied and reflects the region in which the artist lived and the lifestyle of his or her cultural group. The Inuit, for example, carved ivory and soapstone

Bill Reid

Bill Reid is one of Canada's most widely recognized Northwest coast native artists. His work ranges from handmade jewelry to woodcarvings and massive sculptures. Born in 1920 to a father of European descent and a mother of the Haida First Nation, Reid lived most of his life in British Columbia. While working in broadcasting, he studied jewelry making at Ryerson Institute of Technology. A chance visit to the Royal Ontario Museum, where he saw a collection of Northwest coast native art, sparked an interest in his mother's heritage. From that point forward, Reid focused on studying and honoring the art of the Haida. Reid is perhaps best known for *The Spirit of Haida Gwaii*, a large sculpture depicting a canoe full of travelers, some human and some animal, which was inspired by a Haida myth. The work was completed in 1996 and is on display at the Vancouver International Airport.

to create animal and human figurines that were often depicted swimming. The materials and the subject matter reflect their close relationship with and dependence on the animals they harvested from the ocean.

Contemporary Indigenous Art

First Nation artists continue to make art today. However, the creative process has changed drastically since the pre-contact era. Not only has the European aesthetic become much more influential, but the traditional practice of one generation passing on artistic knowledge to the next is all but nonexistent. Although there are small communities who still use traditional methods to create works of art such as totem poles, there are also many indigenous Canadians who use modern materials and manufacturing

Inuit created the soapstone carving in this photograph. Carvings like this one usually depict animals and the activities of the Inuit hunter-gatherer culture. During the 1950s, these carvings became popular with Canadian and international art collectors. Today, there is a worldwide demand for soapstone carvings found in the Arctic northwest.

techniques to make traditional items like masks and boxes, which are then sold at shops specializing in native souvenirs. There are also First Nations whose artistic education comes entirely from attending Canadian universities. Although the artists they study and the mediums with which they work are often rooted in European traditions, the personal statements they make through their art often reflect their indigenous backgrounds.

Creating with a Purpose

The first European artists in Canada were practical. They painted with a specific objective in mind rather than with the intention of creating great works of art. The first English artists went only as far as sketches of the land, which resembled topographic maps. The Catholic Church, for example, encouraged clergymen to produce works that would promote Catholic values. The artistic or creative skill of the painter was not as important as the ability to convey the message. Even as the population grew, Canada's creative culture lagged behind in development, and it wasn't until the middle of the nineteenth century that Canadian painters began to gain local and international recognition.

One of Canada's most well-known early painters was Paul Kane (1810–1871), who lived in what is now Toronto. Kane was an enthusiastic traveler, and he frequently sketched and painted both the Canadian landscape and the indigenous people he came across during his journeys. His paintings were collected and published in a book entitled *Wanderings of an Artist*.

Group of Seven

In the early 1900s, the Canadian art scene exploded with innovation and international recognition with the help of the Group of Seven, a small group of Toronto-based

painters led by J. E. H. MacDonald. Like Kane before them, the Group of Seven traveled the country and were inspired to paint it. In 1920, at an art gallery in Toronto, the Group of Seven had its first exhibit, which was harshly criticized by both art critics and the public. When their paintings were shown in England and Paris, however, they were well received by critics, and they eventually gained acceptance in Canada as well.

In the years to follow, the most dominant art movements in Canada paralleled those of Europe. However, the Canadian government provided little financial support for Canadian artists, which limited the advancements in visual arts among Canadian artists in comparison to their European counterparts.

By the late 1950s, the government established the Canada Council, a government-funded organization whose goal continues to be the advancement of the arts, humanities, and social sciences. The council provides financial assistance to artists and arts organizations.

Often called the purest example of Gothic revival architecture in the Western Hemisphere, namely for the ornamentation of intricate carvings, gargoyles, and towers, the Parliament buildings on Parliament Hill in Ottawa are Canada's most important historical monuments. They are composed of three buildings—Centre, East, and West Block—and were built between 1857 and 1866. The buildings were originally intended to house not only Parliament but the entire Canadian administration.

Jack Bush

Jack Bush was one of Canada's most accomplished painters. He was best known as a founding member of Painters Eleven, a group based in Toronto that wanted to increase the awareness of abstract painting. At first the public responded negatively to his paintings, which featured bold yet simple shapes in vivid colors. Canadians eventually embraced his work and the abstract movement. Bush was born in Toronto in 1909 and raised in Montréal. While working in Canada after graduating high school, he also attended art school and studied under several well-known Canadian artists. After gaining notoriety as an abstract painter with Painters Eleven, Bush experimented with abstract expressionism and color block painting. Bush died in 1977, but he remains a major influence on young Canadian painters.

The 1950s saw the emergence of the Painters Eleven, a group of Toronto-based artists who organized as a group to increase the profile of abstract art. The Painters Eleven were initially met with critical resistance. The Toronto art scene at the time was very much dominated by the Group of Seven and their landscape paintings. Eventually, like that of the Group of Seven before them, the work of the Painters Eleven met with praise in Canada, New York, and overseas.

Today, there are thriving art scenes in all of Canada's major cities, and there are many well-respected public and private galleries. Many of the country's best universities boast excellent fine arts programs. A large part of the unique identity that Canada has been able to forge has its roots in both the inspiring nature of the vast landscape and its artists' willingness to embrace all of the country's resident cultures, especially its most ancient.

Built to Survive

During the early part of Canada's history, architectural design was more a testament to creativity and a will to survive than creating a work of art. Working with limited materials and facing often brutal weather conditions, Canada's indigenous population and the European explorers who followed them built structures that were for the most part sturdy and able to withstand harsh winters.

Although the buildings Canada's indigenous population built were largely functional, that doesn't mean they lacked beauty. Even to this day, one of the most

Open since 1989, the Skydome in Toronto is the world's first sports facility to have a fully retractable roof and serves the city's baseball and football teams. It has the capacity to hold 53,000 spectators, and although many stadiums are now opting for a retractable roof that moves on a linear track, the Skydome remains unique. The architects patented their design of the end cap, which rotates 180 degrees to tuck itself under the other panels.

well known and compelling designs, known not just in Canada, but throughout the world, is the simple yet delightful igloo. Its design perfectly marries the need for shelter with technology and appropriate materials given Canada's environment.

The Haida, a First Nation people who lived on the west coast, lived in permanent settlements and built their homes from split logs, which they painted on the outside, often in colors and designs that matched that of a totem pole. The designs on the house combined with the totem pole served the purpose of giving onlookers information about the status of the household's inhabitants.

The first European houses were strictly functional. They were re-creations of the homes built in the country from which the settlers emigrated. Adjustments were made as needed. For example, the earliest settlers only had to experience one Canadian winter to learn that the roofs on their homes needed to be stronger than those in Europe if they were to withstand the weight of a heavy snowfall. Early forts, churches, and schools were similarly functional in structure.

Today, Canada joins the other countries of the world in aspiring to build monumental structures. Although many of the country's most well known buildings follow the European tradition, many of its most highly praised buildings are much more daring and reflect the country's wide open and often dramatic landscape.

A Design Mosaic

As the population grew and cities developed, Canadian architecture grew more sophisticated. Since the seventeenth century, building design had been dominated by European traditions, first through the French settlers in the seventeenth and eighteenth centuries, then as influenced by the British in the nineteenth century. Today, the homes, offices, and various public buildings in Canada borrow from a wide range of classical and contemporary architectural schools.

Arthur Erickson

Internationally recognized architect Arthur Erickson is best known in Canada for the Burnaby campus of Simon Fraser University in British Columbia, the rebirth of Vancouver's old courthouse as the Vancouver Art Gallery, and the University of British Columbia's Museum of Anthropology. Erickson's designs are noted for their dramatic use of geometric forms and their incorporation of unusual construction materials, including plastic and laminated paper. Erickson was born in Vancouver in 1924. At sixteen, he was honored as the youngest artist to win honorable mention for work entered in a Vancouver Art Gallery exhibit. As a young adult, he was inspired to pursue architecture after studying the work of American architect Frank Lloyd Wright. Fired by two firms for being too experimental, his first successes came with designing homes in the Vancouver region. In the mid-1950s, he took a teaching position with the University of Oregon. Erickson has received numerous awards, including the Gold Medal from the American Institute of Architecture. Today, he presides over Arthur Erickson Architects, a firm based in Vancouver.

Toronto's skyline is dominated by sky-scrapers, high-rise condos, and hotels on the waterfront, with at least fifty buildings that are more than 300 feet (92 meters) tall. Although not a true skyscraper, Old City Hall, a clock tower, is Toronto's most beloved and oldest building. When it was built in 1899, this 340-foot (104-meter) structure was one of the tallest in Toronto.

Among the buildings in Canada praised for their innovative or elegant design are Ottawa's neo-Gothic Parliament buildings, which were completed in 1866, and the Frontenac in Québec City and the Empress in Victoria, two chateau-style hotels that were built in the late 1800s.

Eye-catching modern designs that are uniquely Canadian include the Canadian Museum of Civilization, which was designed by First Nation Douglas Cardinal. The design is noted for its use of smooth round shapes. In the late 1960s, Ray Affleck designed Place Bonaventure, a self-contained city block which houses offices, restaurants, and a hotel, and addresses the problem of severe winter temperatures, which often discourage people from venturing outside their homes and offices.

Art and architecture as designed and created by First Nations have had a long history in Canada. However, it is only in the past century that the cultural contributions of Canada's indigenous population have been viewed as noteworthy by the international art and architecture community. This reaction reflects the prejudices held toward the cultural achievements of pre-European civilizations. In the past century, however, many of Canada's artists and architects have not only received international recognition, but they have also created works of art and designs that speak to Canada's unique mix of cultures.

THE LITERATURE AND MUSIC OF CANADA

8

C anada is a nation that claims two official languages—French and English—thus Canadian literature and music have a mixed and wonderfully rich cultural past. And while French, English, and indigenous art often exist separately from each other, there is also a healthy level of cross-pollination, which is reflected in the unique richness of Canadian literature and music.

Overcoming French and English Dominance

Canadians once thought of themselves as a people without a culture that was distinctly "Canadian." The earliest settlers were occupied with the basic hardships of survival and had little time to develop a written tradition that was uniquely Canadian; theirs was a vibrant oral tradition. Later, settlers told of their difficult lifestyles in books like Susanna Moodie's *Roughing It in the Bush* and *Life Clearings*. Another early pioneer writer, Catharine Parr Traill, wrote similar tales of hardship in *The Backwoods of Canada*.

Members of the Canadian troupe Cirque du Soleil *(left)* perform a chair-balancing act as a part of their show. Originally marking the 450th anniversary celebration of Jacques Cartier's arrival in Canada, actors such as stilt walkers, jugglers, and fire blowers gathered and performed the first Cirque du Soleil. Much different from a traditional circus, Cirque du Soleil is a theatrical show that features an original score, lighting effects, and costumes. Native Indians *(above)* dance at a powwow. Powwows are ceremonies that celebrate family or religious events by singing, dancing, and oral storytelling. This festival is famous for its brightly colored costumes and fast-paced dancing. A powwow usually lasts a weekend and attracts hundreds of visitors from all backgrounds.

A member of the Red Thunder Native Dance Theatre performs the hoop dance at a folk festival in Canmore, Canada. The hoop dance is performed by energetic dancers who maneuver as many as thirty hoops over their body while dancing to fast-paced music. This dance was originally a healing ritual by Canadian Indian and Native American tribes. According to Native American beliefs, each time a dancer passes his body through a hoop, he adds another year to his life.

However, even after permanent settlements were established and new technologies granted Canadians leisure time, French and British literature continued to be recognized more than the work of native Canadian writers. Octave Cremazie, a French Canadian poet, complained that writers in Canada were sometimes less well known for being distinctly Canadian because they were identified by their British and French heritage.

Survival Stories

Canada's first writers were European explorers who wrote about their new surroundings and their interactions with Canada's indigenous population. Jacques Cartier, who led the first European expedition up the St. Lawrence River, wrote an account of his experiences in 1545. To this day, Canada's rugged and imposing environment is often a theme in Canadian literature.

Les Voyages de la Novvelle France, the description of Samuel de Champlain's voyage around Canada to find the Northwest Passage was the last book in a series of four successive titles that documented the life of the navigator and cartographer. Champlain's experience as a colonial administrator documents the events that occurred in New France between 1603 and 1629 and informs historians about colonial life during that time.

LES
VOYAGES
DE LA
NOVVELLE FRANCE
OCCIDENTALE, DICTE
CANADA,
FAITS PAR LE S' DE CHAMPLAIN

In 1760, with the British conquest of New France, the country's French language literature virtually disappeared. The educated elite returned to France in great numbers. French-speaking Canadians lost their writers and teachers, so future French Canadian literature was threatened. However, the French who remained felt strongly about preserving their culture. During the early 1800s, a number of French authors published books on the history of the French in Canada.

English-speaking author Frances Brooke wrote the first internationally known Canadian novel, *The History of Emily Montague,* in 1769. Following in the footsteps of the Canadian writers who had come before her, Brooke centered her book on the theme of survival in a new environment. The challenges of life in a new land would continue as a central theme for many of Canada's fiction writers well into the nineteenth century.

The 1860s saw the formation of the School of Québec, an organization of French poets who often blended themes of nature and patriotism. Later in the 1800s, a group of English poets formed a group called the Confederation Poets, and they, too, wrote poems about the natural world.

Margaret Atwood

Margaret Atwood was born in Ottawa in 1939. She started her career as a poet, publishing *The Circle Game*, which won the Governor General's Award. In 1969, she published a novel, *The Edible Woman*, and continued to publish poetry and fiction while writing literary criticism, history, children's books, television and film scripts, plays, and cartoons. During the early 1970s, Atwood edited two magazines and wrote a guide to Canadian literature that is still widely taught in college literature courses. In 1974, Atwood published *You Are Happy*, which retells *The Odyssey* from the perspective of a female character. In the 1980s, she was appointed vice chair of the Writers' Union of Canada and produced work in a wide variety of mediums, including television, theater, and children's literature. Atwood is best known for her novel *The Handmaid's Tale*, published in 1985. The book takes a searing look at society's tolerance of gender inequality.

The Rise of Canadian Literature

Spurred by World War I, Canadian nationalism rose during the 1920s and 1930s. With this patriotism came a renewed interest in supporting the arts. In 1921, a group of writers founded the Canadian Authors Association, whose purpose was to promote and celebrate Canadian writers. According to *A History of the Canadian People*, between 1920 and 1940, more than 750 Canadian novels were published, many by authors who went on to achieve both national and international recognition.

In the latter half of the twentieth century, Canadian literature truly came of age, producing a great number of distinguished authors whose talents are recognized worldwide. Sinclair Ross's *As for Me and My House*, which tells of the difficulty of Canadian prairie life during the Great Depression, was widely acclaimed.

Canadian Malcolm Lowry authored *Under the Volcano*, a classic in English fiction.

During the 1960s and 1970s, the landscape of Canada became more urban, and literature followed suit. In a shift away from traditional rural and naturalistic themes, Hugh MacLennan wrote *The Watch that Ends the Night*, a novel set in Montréal that examines Canada's moral and political values.

Ancient Songs and Dances

On a national level, Canada has always had a strong folk music scene. For thousands of years, music and dance have been integral parts of the lives of Canada's indigenous people, and despite attempts by settlers to obliterate the native culture, they still thrive today. First Nations not only continue to perform the music and dance of their ancestors as part of their own religious observations and celebrations, but they also perform for the public in a variety of forums.

Canadian author, script-writer, and essayist Mordecai Richler (1931–2001) began his career as a freelance journalist in London, England. He was born in Montréal and attended Sir George Williams University. He returned to Montréal in 1972 and published many novels and screenplays, as well as two children's books. His work is typically set in the Canadian Jewish community and is well known for its open sarcasm and strong criticism toward supporters of the Québec separatist movement.

The most well known native dance of the Arctic people of Canada is drum dancing, largely performed at festivals to honor the deceased. Dancers form a semicircle and use their arms and upper body to express feelings and emotions, while drummers create the rhythm and sing along.

Modern Canadian folk music has its roots in the songs of the First Nations and has evolved over centuries with the introduction of each new wave of immigrants. Folk music has flourished because Canadians enjoy traditional music festivals, which bring together well-known folk singers from a wide variety of cultures. Each year, thousands travel to New Brunswick, a stronghold of Irish immigrants, to attend a festival that boasts the largest number of Irish musicians and dancers outside of Ireland. In addition, there are folk musicians and storytellers from all over the world. In other regions, popular folk music reflects the European population that settled there years ago. In Québec, where French culture dominates, festivals often feature folk music that can trace its stylistic and thematic roots to France.

Seeking a Distinct Voice

Though the music of Canada's indigenous people has long been a vital part of the national music scene, European colonization played a distinct and often

Canadian singer Robert Charlebois is one of Canada's most talented playwrights and vocalists. He was born in 1944 and from an early age devoted himself to both theater and music. His career took off by 1965 with his well-received play *Yéyés vs Chansonnier* and his first award-winning album, *Charlebois Vol.1*. Charlebois was first propelled to fame in Québec and has contributed to many of Canada's most-loved works.

overwhelming role in the cultural development of the country. Settlers from France and England taught their children to sing and play European instruments. As with other cultural pursuits, development of a unique, national music style was slow in Canada during the 1700s and 1800s, because the population was sparse and isolated from one another, and the settlers were focused on survival. However, while there were few organized performances during this period, music remained an important part of church services, which many Canadians attended.

As the population expanded, the availability of music for purposes of entertainment increased. Regional amateur bands played at parades and organized dances. Not until well into the nineteenth century was it possible for a musician to make a career out of playing music.

By the second half of the nineteenth century, music was taught in most schools, and during this same period, it became possible to obtain a degree in music at several Canadian universities. With a generation of musicians born, raised, and schooled in Canada, it became possible for Canadians to create music with a distinctly Canadian voice. The development of the steamship and railway during this period also meant that an increasing number of both Canadian and European musicians were able to perform and influence one another throughout the country.

National Ballet of Canada performers Johan Persson and Martine Lamy dance during a performance of James Kudelka's *Washington Square*. As a Canadian choreographer, Kudelka is internationally renowned for his ability to create original modern choreography that is influenced by classical dance movements. Kudelka began his career while still a student at the National Ballet School in Toronto.

Modern Music and Dance

In the past century, Canadian musicians have made important strides in creating a musical voice that is distinctly Canadian. From coast to coast, Canada is filled with talented musicians who have contributed to a variety of musical genres including classical, jazz, folk, country, rock, and popular music.

Today, Canada has several outstanding orchestras, including the Montréal Symphony Orchestra, the National Arts Centre Orchestra, the Toronto Symphony Orchestra, and the Vancouver Symphony Orchestra. Canadian Glen Gould is a leader within the genre as one of Canada's most talented classical pianists.

Each summer, Montréal holds a jazz festival that is world renowned for the talent it gathers. Well-known Canadian jazz musicians include Oscar Peterson and

Bramwell Tovey conducts the Vancouver Symphony Orchestra and more than 6,000 student musicians as they perform for a campaign advocating the benefits of music education for young people. The Vancouver Symphony Orchestra is the third-largest orchestra in Canada and regularly provides workshops and programs to educate youngsters in music instruction and appreciation.

Alanis Morissette

Alanis Morissette was born in 1974, in Ottawa. She burst onto the international pop music scene in 1995, with the release of her third album, *Jagged Little Pill*, which has sold 30 million units worldwide and was voted Album of the Decade by *Billboard* magazine. Once a child

actress, Morissette released two dance albums prior to *Jagged Little Pill* and enjoyed modest success. Hoping to evolve in a more serious musical direction, Morissette moved to Los Angeles to work on the material for her third release. The song "You Oughta Know," which captured Morissette's bitter response to a breakup, caught the attention of international listeners. Morissette released a fourth record, *Supposed Former Infatuation Junkie*, in 1998. Though not as popular as her third release, it was still well received by both fans and critics. Since then, Morissette has taken acting roles, most memorably playing the part of God in the American movie *Dogma*.

Maynard Ferguson, who was inducted into the Jazz Educators Hall of Fame in 1992. Canada also has a very strong folk music scene with multitalented artists that include Leonard Cohen, Joni Mitchell, and Sarah McLachlan.

Celine Dion began singing at the age of five and recorded her first songs at age twelve. Although her albums sold very well in Canada, France, and Switzerland, she was still largely unknown in the United States until she began singing in English during the late 1980s.

Pop Music Explodes

In recent years, Canada has made some important strides in gaining national recognition of its popular musicians, among them Celine Dion. Much has been made of Dion's humble beginnings in the small town of Charlemagne, Québec, where she grew up speaking French. Dion's first brush with international fame came in France, where she was the first Canadian singer to have a gold record. Country singer Shania Twain's Canadian upbringing has been similarly celebrated.

Other internationally known Canadians perform within a wide variety of popular music genres. Musical styles range from the rock of Neil Young to the pure pop performed by Nelly Furtardo and Avril Lavigne.

Since World War II, Canada's authors and musicians have come into their own. With its own rich pool of creative talent, Canada no longer need depend on the latest trends from either Europe or the United States. In an effort to nurture its own talent, the Canadian government requires that Canadian artists comprise at least 35 percent of radio station programming. French-language radio stations must ensure that at least 65 percent of the popular music selections they broadcast each week are in the French language.

FAMOUS FOODS AND RECIPES OF CANADA

9

T he typical Canadian diet reflects the European background of most of its residents. In the cities of Québec and Montréal, where French culture dominates, popular dishes are often interpretations of recipes in France. Tastes vary from region to region and are often influenced by the availability of foodstuffs. On either coast, fish is more popular, while Canadians living in the central part of the country tend to eat more meat.

In addition to the foods that most Canadians cook in their own homes, there are a wide variety of nationalities represented in Canada's many restaurants. Chinese food is particularly popular throughout Canada, as is Italian cuisine. Again, there are regional differences that represent the tendency of immigrants of the same nationality to settle in the same city or province. In Toronto, for example, Sri Lankan restaurants are common because there is a high percentage of Sri Lankans living there.

Much like its people, Canadian food represents a mix of cultures from around the world. There are, however, some foods and dishes that are distinctly Canadian.

Canadian Cuisine

Canada is bordered by three different oceans—the Atlantic, the Arctic, and the Pacific—and some of the foods for which the country is best known are harvested from these

Fishermen in this photograph *(left)* bring in their latest catch. Canada's location on the Arctic, Atlantic, and Pacific Oceans, as well as its border along the Great Lakes, gives the country the world's longest coastline. Canada's fishing industry is worth more than $5 billion per year. Canadians in this photograph *(above)* dine along Rue Prince Arthur in Montréal. Many Canadians eat one large meal a day that consists of meat, potatoes, and vegetables.

This Canadian Cree trapper checks his fishnet. The food that Canadians eat often depends on where they live. On Canada's eastern coast, lobster, scallops, and fiddlehead greens, an edible fern, are popular. In Newfoundland, cod tongues and seal flipper are the ingredients in many recipes. *Tourtière* (meat pie) and *tarte au sucre* (sugar pie) are favorite foods in Québec, while in the north, people eat seal blubber and Arctic char, a type of fish.

chilly waters. In Newfoundland, which was first settled because of its proximity to the abundant waters of the Atlantic Ocean, fish is an important part of the diet. Shellfish populate the waters more so than any other fish, so much so that the province's most popular dishes contain oysters, clams, and mussels.

Nova Scotia and British Columbia are famous for their salmon, which travel from the ocean and navigate up rivers and streams to breed in the cool waters of the two provinces' many lakes. Salmon season starts in early September and ends on October 31. Canadians throughout the country are very fond of salmon that is lightly salted and smoked, known as lox. And while the number of salmon harvested now is much lower than in the past, Nova Scotia is so well known for its lox that the term "Nova lox" is now used generically to describe salted and smoked salmon.

Visit any one of New Brunswick's or Prince Edward Island's popular seafood restaurants and you are sure to find clam chowder on the menu. The chowder is a thick, rich soup of clams, which are harvested in the Atlantic Ocean.

Nanaimo Bars

Nanaimo bars are a sweet treat enjoyed throughout Canada. They are named after the city in British Columbia where they first became popular.

Ingredients:

Base
1 cup melted butter
   (2 sticks)
½ cup granulated sugar
1 cup unsweetened cocoa
2 eggs, beaten
3 cups graham
   cracker crumbs
1 cup coconut flakes
1 cup chopped walnuts

Middle Layer
½ cup butter (1 stick),
   at room temperature
4 tablespoons custard
   powder (or substitute
   instant vanilla Jello
   pudding powder)
2 teaspoons vanilla
3 tablespoons milk
2 cups confectioner's sugar

Icing
8 ounces semisweet
   chocolate
4 ounces unsweetened
   chocolate
3 tablespoons butter

18–24 Servings

Base: Mix together melted butter and sugar. Stir in cocoa, then eggs. Beat until smooth. Add graham cracker crumbs; mix thoroughly. Stir in coconut and walnuts. Press into two 9-inch square pans. Refrigerate while making middle layer.

Middle Layer: Cream together butter, custard powder, and vanilla. Gradually blend in milk and confectioner's sugar. Spread evenly over base. Chill well before icing.

Icing: Melt chocolates and butter together on low heat. Spread onto chilled middle layer. Chill in a refrigerator, but cut into pieces before the chocolate on top has completely hardened. Store in the refrigerator in an airtight container.

This woman sells maple syrup in Montréal. Before Europeans arrived in Canada, native Canadians had perfected the formula for making maple syrup. When Europeans came to the continent, they used this relatively inexpensive sweetener instead of importing sugar from other countries. Since then, the province of Québec has become the top producer of maple sugar and maple products in the world.

By Way of France

In Québec, the dominant culture is French, and the food of the region reflects this heritage. There are also a number of hybridized dishes, which combine French cooking techniques with regional ingredients. Perhaps the most famous Québec dish of all is *poutine*, a very simple and very greasy dish. Simply take one bowl of French fries, cover it with a handful of cheddar cheese curds, and then top with beef gravy.

Tourtiere is a French Canadian meat pie that is often cooked with pork and traditionally served on Christmas Eve after midnight mass. Québec is also well known for its wide assortment of cheeses, especially Oka, a soft, flavored cheese made by monks who live in the province.

Desserts

During the spring in Québec and Ontario, maple syrup is harvested, or "sugared off," a process which is usually celebrated as a social event. The syrup is often dripped on

Children tour a maple sugar shack in a traditional Québec pioneer village in Rigaud. Sugar shacks can be found throughout the winter forests of Québec. The winter cold holds the sap in its frozen state, and in the spring, the sap melts and drips into a can hanging beneath the tap. When the sap runs, children pick up and lick the sticky substance with twigs or fingers before it is processed into maple syrup.

clean snow for children to snack on and enjoy. Maple syrup is not only used as a topping for pancakes and waffles but also as an ingredient in a wide variety of sweet treats, including cakes, candies, and cookies. Saskatoon berries are a sweet fruit native to Saskatchewan. There they are a common ingredient in pies and jams.

Ice wine is a sweet alcoholic drink that adults often enjoy after dinner. Most often produced in Québec, ice wine is made by harvesting the grapes after the first frost hits. These grapes are then pressed while still frozen, which makes for a highly concentrated and sweet juice.

The Canadian baker in this photograph shows off her sweet wares. Springtime in Québec gives rise to many meals made with maple sugar collected from the maple trees' sap. Foods and beverages that are unique to French Canadians include maple sugar pie, maple sugar candies, maple liquor, and maple coffee.

DAILY LIFE AND CUSTOMS IN CANADA

10

As Canada leaves behind the twentieth century and begins the new millennium, the way in which its people live is slowly changing. About half of all Canadians above the age of fifteen are married. However, this number has been slowly decreasing for many years because more Canadian couples are waiting to get married or choosing to live together but remain unmarried.

According to Statistics Canada, the percentage of Canadians living as "traditional" families continues to decline, while the number of children living with one parent is on the rise. An increasing proportion of unmarried couples are also living together. These common-law families accounted for 14 percent of all families in 2001, up from 6 percent in 1981. The 2001 census is the first to provide data on same-sex partnerships. In total, 34,200 couples identified themselves as same-sex common-law couples, and most of them were male.

In the 1960s and 1980s, changes in Canada's divorce laws made it easier for couples to seek a divorce, and the number of divorces increased dramatically. In recent years, the divorce rate has stabilized.

Canadians *(left)* walk and ice-skate on the frozen Rideau Canal in Ottawa. The Rideau Canal, originally built in the nineteenth century to provide a safe supply route between Montréal and the Great Lakes, is North America's oldest operating canal. It's now a popular tourist attraction, especially in the winter when 5 miles (8 km) are cleared to become the longest outdoor skating rink in the world. A child *(above)* plays with her puppy. Canada's cold temperatures give pleasure to many youngsters who often spend hours in activities associated with winter sports, such as sledding, snowboarding, skiing, and ice-skating.

The young Canadian girl in this photograph completes a school assignment. A recent survey shows that an increasing number of students are doing their homework online. Canadian teenagers spend approximately 2.4 hours per week conducting online research for the purposes of education.

A Youthful Existence

In 1986, roughly 21 percent of Canada's population was under the age of fifteen. Since the early 1800s, there has been a shift from viewing children as capable laborers to a demographic in need of both adult protection and an extended period of education.

A closer look at Canada's teen population says much about the country's social and cultural values. Though teens worldwide are often stereotyped as troublemakers, Canadian teens break the mold. According to an article in *Transition* magazine, the percentage of teens who volunteer almost doubled between 1987 and 1997, growing from 18 percent to 33 percent. Also, today's Canadian teens are very concerned with finding jobs as adults, and as a result, they are staying in school longer.

Although they may seem serious when compared to their American or European counterparts, Canadian teens still like to have fun. Spending time with friends and shopping at the mall are still favorite activities, though in recent years Canadian teens have been spending more time on their computers.

Ice hockey is Canada's national game. Canadian children, who often learn the sport when they are very young, normally participate in leagues hosted by local rinks. Almost every Canadian town has a hockey team, and the larger cities have professional teams. Watching hockey is a tradition in many Canadian households during the winter season.

At the beginning of the twenty-first century, Canadian teens committed fewer crimes than the generation before them. But today's teens are committing more violent crimes than teens in the past.

An Aging Society

Canada's population is aging. By the year 2011, it is predicted that only 16 percent of the population will be under the age of fifteen. Even now, according to criteria established by the United Nations, Canada is defined as possessing an aged population, which means that more than 8 percent of its people are sixty-five years of age or older. There is much concern among Canadians that it will become increasingly difficult, given the decreasing ratio of workers to retirees, for the government to support the numerous social programs geared toward the elderly. In recent years, there has been talk of increasing the amount of money workers must contribute to pension funds, cutting benefits, and curtailing retirement.

Most of Canada's elderly live in private households, with just 9 percent residing in nursing homes. Some provinces impose a mandatory retirement age, meaning that those residents above a certain age are required to retire. Canadians have an average life expectancy of seventy-four years of age for men and eighty years for women, so it is not surprising that Canada's elderly population tends to stay active after retirement, participating in sports activities, learning new hobbies, taking college classes, and volunteering.

Canadians have a strong sense of family values; however, the Canadian definition of family has been changing over the past several decades. Currently, 13 percent of all Canadian families are single-parent households. Other extended families include grandparents, cousins, or other relatives. Sometimes adult children remain in the family home rather than start independent households.

The Shift from Rural to Urban

As was the case for most nations of the world, early Canadian society was rural, and its people were very much dependent on the land both for subsistence and commerce. Today, the vast majority of Canadians live in urban areas. This shift began in the 1940s, with the rise of manufacturing and service industries in Canada's cities. Now, according to Statistics Canada, 78 percent of the population live in an urban area, 19 percent live in a rural region, and 3 percent live on a farm.

Canadians are engaged in every modern employment, but certain industries are limited by geography and climate. Regardless of location, the majority of the population works for the government, a service industry, or a manufacturer. A very small percentage of Canadians still lives on farms, where their existence has been greatly changed by the advent of modern machinery.

In the Arctic, Inuit and other First Nations, many of whom still follow their traditional occupations as fishers and hunters, dominate the population. They, too, have experienced the influence of modernization, however. The food they eat, the clothes they wear, and the equipment they use in their everyday lives have been adapted to modern conditions.

The Effects of Class

In 1998, according to Statistics Canada, the average income for a two-parent family with children was $55,074, which was close to a 9 percent increase over the average income in 1993. In recent years, Canadians have benefited from a healthy economy in which the unemployment rate dropped from 9.5 percent in 1997 to 7.3 percent in 2003.

Unlike the United States, Canada does not have an official poverty line, but Statistics Canada defines a low-income family as earning less than half of the median family income. Using that definition, the poverty level has increased over the past twenty-five years, though in recent years it has dropped in some groups because of the healthy economy. Poverty rates are highest in Canada among single mothers, First Nations, visible minorities, and persons with disabilities.

Most of Canada's raw materials are processed before they are exported. Trees, for example, are cut into shingles, made into lumber, or used to make pulp and paper products. Canada is the world's leading exporter of forest products, accounting for 21 percent of their trade in the entire world and sending those products to more than one hundred countries.

EDUCATION AND WORK IN CANADA

11

T he lifestyle and life stages of the average Canadian are similar to those experienced in most developed nations. Children do not work. Instead, they are required to attend school until their mid-teens. Upon graduation from high school, children are generally encouraged by their parents and elders to attend college rather than enter the workforce. As adults, both men and women work, though women more often work part-time, and women who have young children often choose to focus on their roles as caregiver. Canadians generally like to relax at home on the weekends when they are not attending school or work. They also enjoy friend and family get-togethers and will often take short trips to enjoy Canada's beautiful countryside. Canadians stop working in their mid-sixties. Senior citizens enjoy living independent lifestyles and generally stay relatively active for years to come.

Emphasis on Education

Since the early 1800s, Canada has been committed to the principle of publicly funded systems of education. Children must attend school from the ages of six to fifteen. State-sponsored schools offer an excellent education free of cost, and students are free to attend private schools as well.

This woman *(left)* browses through a flea market in Brocanteur, Canada. Many towns have a variety of shopping outlets that sell both new and used goods. Malls, boutiques, and antique shops can be found in just about every Canadian neighborhood. The farmer in this photograph *(above)* feeds pigs, sheep, and geese from the back of a pickup truck. Although the agricultural workers in Canada represent a small segment of its total population, the agricultural industry is an important sector of the nation's economy. New technologies have revolutionized Canada's farming methods. These include better pesticides, fertilizer, and herbicides, improved harvesting techniques, and genetic advancements in plant and animal production.

Canada spends more money on education than most other Western nations. Each province in Canada is responsible for its own educational system, but it is federally mandated that all Canadian children attend school for at least eight years. Public education is free until the end of secondary school, but some provinces require children to purchase their own textbooks.

After one year of kindergarten, children attend eight years of elementary school followed by four years of secondary school. The school year begins in the first week of September and ends in June, and children attend school Monday through Friday from about 9:00 AM to 3:00 PM. In elementary school, the curriculum is centered on providing a solid foundation in reading, writing, and mathematics.

In all provinces except Québec, where classes are taught in French, children in elementary and secondary school are taught in English. In some provinces, French-speaking children have the right to be taught in French.

Teens are encouraged to attend college when they graduate from high school, and some 75 percent of Canadian high school students do, which is the highest percentage in the industrialized world. In order to attend college, students must meet specific entrance requirements, which vary according to the college or university. Unlike the publicly funded elementary and secondary schools, colleges and universities charge tuition and often room and board as well. Students can obtain a bachelor of arts or bachelor of

About 45 percent of new Canadian jobs created in the future will require at least sixteen years of education. All provinces have their own universities, which are funded by the government and student tuition. The Canadian educational system has contributed to a successful literacy rate of 99 percent.

science degree after attending college for four years, but many students work and attend school part-time and as a result take longer to earn their degrees.

There are close to eighty universities in Canada and more than two hundred higher education institutes. They range in size from those with fewer than one thousand students to those with as many as twenty-five thousand students. In most universities, classes are given in English, but in colleges and universities in Québec, students are taught in French. Throughout Canada, there are a handful of bilingual universities.

Obtaining a good education has been given increasing emphasis, and since the early 1970s, the number of Canadians earning at least a high school diploma has doubled. According the 1996 census, many of those students went on to college, and 16 percent of the population over the age of fifteen had already obtained a university degree.

The Working World

There are approximately 15 million Canadians in the workforce, a number that has grown steadily since the start of the twentieth century, in large part because of immigration. Sixty percent of employed Canadians live in either Ontario or Québec. Canadians are legally able to start working when they are fifteen. However, as more high school students choose to attend college, the number of teen workers has declined.

The twentieth century has seen a dramatic increase in the number of working women. Once a small percentage of Canada's total number of workers, women now make up about half of Canada's working population.

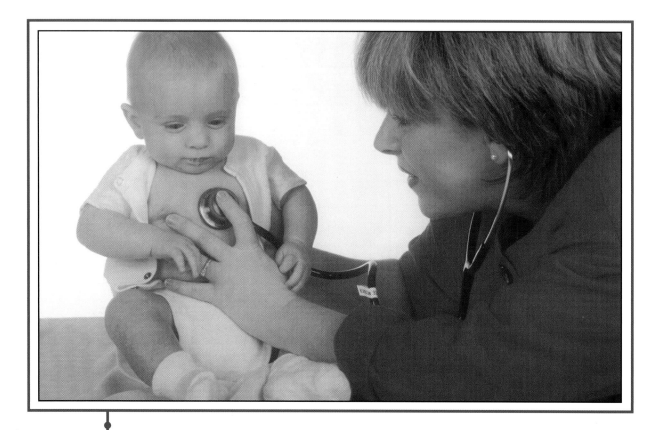

Most women and First Nation workers have incomes significantly lower than the country's overall average. Women tend to make about 15 percent less than men for equivalent work, and for the country's indigenous people, that inequality is even greater.

The typical workday in Canada begins at around 9 AM and continues until 5 PM, Monday through Friday. Many workers, especially those in the service industries, may work at night and on the weekends. Many Canadians also hold part-time jobs for which they work approximately twenty hours a week and often have evening and weekend schedules.

What Canadians Do for a Living

European explorers originally came to Canada in search of natural resources. For many years after the arrival of the Europeans, the country's workforce was largely occupied with taking advantage of Canada's considerable natural resources.

Canadian children are often independent. According to statistics compiled by the Canadian Fitness and Research Institute, more than half of all school-aged children (52%) were enrolled in after-school programs in 2002, while a significant number of others worked part-time jobs.

There are still Canadians employed in the farming, mining, and logging industries, collectively known as the primary industries. However, since the end of World War II, the number of Canadians whose work is connected to the processing of natural resources has diminished rapidly. There are, however, still a small percentage of workers who work in the farming, fishing, mining, and lumbering industries. For the most part, they live in Canada's rural regions. Today, many more Canadians work for the government, in manufacturing, or for the service industry sector. There is also a growing number of Canadians who have home-based businesses.

As the number of Canadians working in resource-based industries has declined, so has the number of people working in manufacturing, currently tabulated at slightly more than 15 percent. Major manufacturing

This man shovels a pathway around Parliament Hill in Ottawa. On a typical day for both the senators and members of the House, these government officials meet with their colleagues, the media, and members of the public, and prepare speeches for the chamber, review documents for the work in their committees, and respond to correspondence. To ensure the functioning of Parliament, an administrative staff is employed to distribute information on the agenda, status, and minutes of the Senate and House of Commons.

centers exist in the southern portion of Ontario and in Toronto, which is known for its automobile and steel factories. Toronto is also developing a reputation for its burgeoning high-tech manufacturing industry.

Canada's fastest-growing employment sector is the service industry. Almost 70 percent of Canadians are involved in service jobs, ranging from work in restaurants and hotels to management consultancy. A growing number of Canadians have started home-based service-oriented businesses, which are often small one- or two-person operations that are run in a person's home.

At the age of sixty-five, many Canadians choose to retire, and for employees of some companies, retirement is mandatory at this time. The Canadian government provides a pension to Canadians sixty-five years of age and older who have lived in the country for at least forty years after the age of eighteen. In the past two decades, the average income of Canada's senior citizens has risen faster than that of people under age sixty-five. Between 1981 and 1997, for example, the average income for seniors rose 18 percent. In contrast, the average income of people aged fifteen to sixty-four has declined 3 percent during the same period.

However, seniors still have lower average incomes than people in most age groups under sixty-five. In 1997, seniors had average incomes of slightly more than $20,000, compared with incomes of well more than $30,000 among people between the ages of thirty-five and fifty-four, and compared with an average of more than $26,000 earned by those in the twenty-five to thirty-four and fifty-five to sixty-four age ranges. Seniors, however, do have a higher average income than fifteen- to twenty-four-year-olds, who averaged just more than $10,000 annually.

Taking a Break

One of the greatest advantages of living in a country as vast as Canada is that there are a variety of landscapes to explore and enjoy. Most Canadians make a habit of

A growing trend in Canadian families is known as the "sandwich generation." This term refers to middle-aged men and women who still have children at home, but who also have elderly parents in the home in need of assistance. Approximately one-fourth of Canada's population is expected to be a part of this growing national trend.

In Canada, many parents work full-time outside of the home and the children are cared for during the day by grandparents or other family members, neighbors, baby-sitters, or daycare agencies.

taking weekend trips as often as possible to visit the mountains, forests, and lakes for which their country is so renowned.

Canada's government is well known for its efforts to protect the environment from development and pollution, and as a result, many of Canada's most beautiful outdoor regions have been set aside as protected national parklands. While visiting these pristine wilderness reserves, Canadians enjoy canoeing, hunting, fishing, hiking, and camping. In addition to planned activities, visitors to the country can almost always count on witnessing some of Canada's abundant wildlife, including caribou, moose, bears, and beavers.

Canadian winters are long, cold, and often snowy, which explains why winter sports such as skiing, sleighing, and ice-skating are all common activities. In Canada, ice-skating is particularly popular, especially among young boys who grow up with dreams of playing for the Canadian National Hockey League. Throughout the year, Canadians also enjoy basketball, baseball, tennis, and lacrosse.

Canadians believe in working hard to achieve goals, whether in work or in school. Though dramatic economic disparities exist along lines of gender, race, and age, Canadians believe in the philosophy that all people are capable of achieving great things, should they put their minds to it. Canadians like to relax, too, and they try hard to live a balanced life, enjoying friends, family, and free time.

Nathan Phillips Square in front of Toronto's City Hall serves as an ice-skating rink during the winter. Ice-skating is a popular winter activity that many Canadians participate in for pleasure and to keep in shape.

CANADA
AT A GLANCE

HISTORY

The first immigrants arrived in Canada about 15,000 years ago. Their descendants first settled the Arctic regions and eventually created settlements throughout modern Canada. Now known as the First Nations, these people spoke a wide variety of languages, and their communities often reflected the climate and the natural resources on which they depended.

Many of the First Nations who settled near the coast were fishermen, while the lifestyle of those people in the interior was more nomadic. In more temperate regions of the country, First Nations also cultivated plants. Often divided along language lines, the numerous First Nation cultural groups sometimes fought over territorial rights, though more often they were tolerant of each other and frequently traded valuable resources.

The first Europeans arrived in Canada in the late tenth or early eleventh century. They were Scandinavian fishermen now known as Vikings or Norsemen. Although they were able to trade with the First Nations who lived on the east coast, their attempts to permanently settle the land were thwarted. The next Europeans arrived during the fifteenth century and settled the continent permanently. Great Britain planted the first flag in Canadian soil, though it was the French who first explored the Canadian interior.

For many years after the arrival of the English, there were numerous conflicts among the French, English, and First Nations over territorial rights. At the conclusion of the Seven Years' War in the mid-1700s, England was able to establish its dominance, though the French were able to maintain a high level of influence on the government.

During the 1800s, Canada's population grew quickly, and in 1841, the British Parliament passed the Act of Union, which united Canada into one colony. By then, European immigrants had settled the country from coast to coast, and as their numbers grew, the First Nation population shrunk, decimated by warfare and disease.

In 1867, the British Parliament approved the British North American Act, which granted Canada the right to self-government. Britain would continue to handle the colony's foreign affairs, and the British monarch served as Canada's head of state.

The twentieth century saw large numbers of Europeans arriving at Canada's shores. The country grew quickly and began to move away from an economy based on natural resources to one centered on manufacturing.

In the second part of the twentieth century, the country once again grappled with conflicts between French- and English-speaking Canadians. Canada's best-known prime minister, Pierre Elliott Trudeau, who held office from 1968 until 1984, was able to keep Canada united despite several strong bids by Québec to become a sovereign nation. Trudeau was also responsible for the Constitution Act of 1982, which ended British control over amendments to Canada's constitution.

Over the past thirty years, Canada has also seen the face of its population change as immigration has increased dramatically. Familiar with the many issues that can arise over cultural clashes, the Canadian government has made it a priority to help new immigrants.

In an effort to improve relations with the first immigrants to Canada, in the late 1990s, Canada established a new territory called Nunavut. Located in the eastern portion of the Northwest Territories, it provides more self-government for the Inuit First Nations, who make up most of its population.

ECONOMY

Canada's economy has evolved quickly from one that was dependent on natural resources to a world power best known for its manufacturing and service industries. Canada's economy is based on privately owned free enterprise and reflects the capitalistic ideals and trading patterns of most Western nations. The Canadian government also plays a significant part in the economy, in that it is involved in regulating many economic activities and owns a wide variety of businesses. It is also responsible for setting policies and collecting taxes, which, in addition to supporting government-run agencies, also affects the ways in which companies run their businesses.

Currently, Canada's gross national product (GNP), which is the total value of the goods and services a country produces, is within the top ten in the world. More than two-thirds of Canada's GNP is generated by the service industries and the other third results from the industrial sector. A very small percentage of the country's GNP results from the agricultural industry.

The service industry not only generates the largest portion of Canada's GNP, it is also the fastest growing industry in Canada. Tourism, education, and health care are three of its major sectors.

Canada is rich in natural resources, which are either exported in their raw form or further processed and then distributed. Canada is a top exporter of fish and furs. Minerals are also important to the country's economy, and Canada is the world's largest producer of zinc and uranium. Canada is also well known for its production of hydroelectricity.

A large part of the country's income is derived from the manufacturing industry, which is best known for iron and steel construction, machinery and equipment production, and telecommunications. Plastics, chemical, and food production are also significant. Furthermore, Japan, South Korea, and the United States operate automobile manufacturing plants in Canada. Aircraft manufacturing is one of the country's fastest-growing industries.

Within its shrinking agricultural industry, Canada is still responsible for a significant percentage of the world's beef cattle, milk, hog, and chicken production. Canada is also one of the world's largest exporters of wheat. Most of Canada's agricultural production takes place in the prairie provinces. Saskatchewan produces about half of the country's wheat, and the rest is grown in Alberta and Manitoba.

Throughout its history, the United States has had a significant effect on the economic health of Canada. America is not only Canada's main trading partner, but it also owns in part or whole some of Canada's largest corporations.

In 1989, Canada entered into the North American Free Trade Agreement, which expanded trade between Canada, the United States, and Mexico by eliminating all taxes on imports. In addition to the United States and Mexico, other important trading partners with Canada include China, Germany, Japan and the United Kingdom.

GOVERNMENT AND POLITICS

Canada's government is described as a parliamentary democracy, a form of government that combines a federal form of government with a monarch, a Senate, and a House of Commons. The federal form of government, which was patterned after the United States, is composed of a union of states or provinces, which recognizes the sovereignty of a central government, while retaining certain powers to govern itself.

Distinct from the United States, Canada's legislative and executive branches of the government reflect a cabinet system much like that of Great Britain. Its main components are the Parliament, the prime minister, and the cabinet. A member of the British Commonwealth, Canada's government also includes a head of state, who is also the monarch of Great Britain.

The Parliament includes two divisions, the Senate and the House of Commons. The Senate includes 105 members, who are appointed by the governor general as recommended by the prime minister. The Parliament meets in a building on Parliament Hill, which is located in Ottawa, Québec.

The 301 members of the House of Commons are voted into office by the Canadian people. Each member represents a different constituency. The number of members is determined by each province's population. If a province has more people, it will have more members in the House of Commons. In fairness to very sparsely populated regions, every province or territory must have at least as many members in the Commons as it has in the Senate.

The House of Commons is responsible for making the laws that affect national policy. The Senate has the power to block passage of bills passed in the House, but it rarely does. The House of Commons also appoints the prime minister of Canada, who is a member of the House of Commons and the leader of the most dominant political party.

The prime minister may hold office for as long as he or she is able to legislatively lead the House of Commons. Should the House of Commons vote down an important bill championed by the prime minister, or if it passes a vote of no confidence, the prime minister either resigns or calls for a general election.

Members of the House of Commons run for office as members of a political party. Although there have been a number of political parties throughout Canada's history, the three most dominant parties are now the Liberal Party, the Reform Party, and the Parti Québécois, which is one that promotes sovereignty for Québec.

In 1867, Canada became the first colony to become a member of the Commonwealth (then called the British Commonwealth). Today, the fifty-three countries that are members of the Commonwealth recognize the king or queen of Great Britain. As such, Queen Elizabeth II is currently recognized as Canada's official head of state and its queen.

TIMELINE

15000 BC

First explorers arrive in Canada via Beringia.

1000 BC

Vikings attempt to create settlements in what is now known as Canada.

AD 1498

Explorers whose trip is sponsored by Great Britain reach the shores of North America.

1841

British Parliament passes the Act of Union, which unites Upper and Lower Canada into the Province of Canada.

1866

Transatlantic cable is laid from Newfoundland to Europe.

1868

Americans purchase Alaska from Russia.

1867

The British North American Act establishes the Dominion of Canada.

1900

Art Museum of Toronto is founded.

1962

The Front de Liberation du Québec, a separatist party, is founded.

1964

New Canadian flag featuring red maple leaf is adopted.

1972

Pierre Elliott Trudeau, representing the Liberal Party, wins a close election.

1969

Through the Official Languages Act, Canada becomes officially a bilingual nation.

1980

Voters in Québec reject proposal to give provincial leaders authority to negotiate with government for sovereignty.

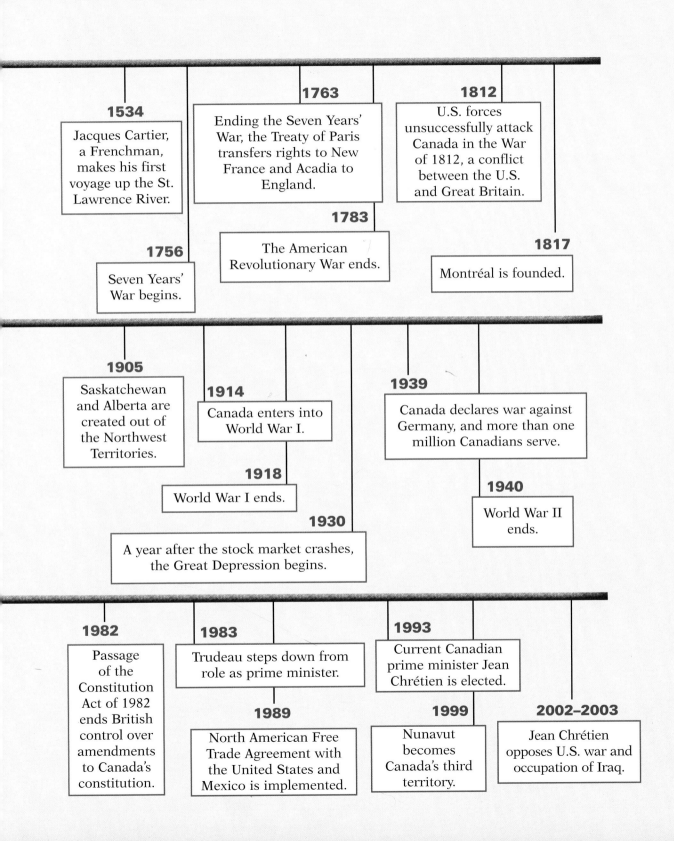

1534
Jacques Cartier, a Frenchman, makes his first voyage up the St. Lawrence River.

1756
Seven Years' War begins.

1763
Ending the Seven Years' War, the Treaty of Paris transfers rights to New France and Acadia to England.

1783
The American Revolutionary War ends.

1812
U.S. forces unsuccessfully attack Canada in the War of 1812, a conflict between the U.S. and Great Britain.

1817
Montréal is founded.

1905
Saskatchewan and Alberta are created out of the Northwest Territories.

1914
Canada enters into World War I.

1918
World War I ends.

1930
A year after the stock market crashes, the Great Depression begins.

1939
Canada declares war against Germany, and more than one million Canadians serve.

1940
World War II ends.

1982
Passage of the Constitution Act of 1982 ends British control over amendments to Canada's constitution.

1983
Trudeau steps down from role as prime minister.

1989
North American Free Trade Agreement with the United States and Mexico is implemented.

1993
Current Canadian prime minister Jean Chrétien is elected.

1999
Nunavut becomes Canada's third territory.

2002–2003
Jean Chrétien opposes U.S. war and occupation of Iraq.

CANADA

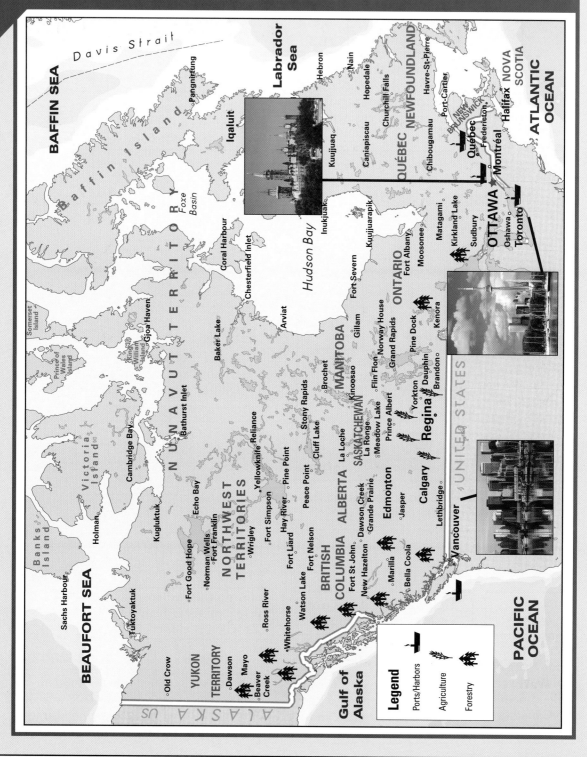

Davis Strait

BAFFIN SEA

Labrador Sea

Baffin Island

BAFFIN SEA

Pangnirtung

Iqaluit

Hebron

Nain

Hopedale

Churchill Falls

Caniapiscau

Kuujjuaq

NEWFOUNDLAND

Havre-St-Pierre

Port-Cartier

NEW BRUNSWICK

Fredericton

Halifax

NOVA SCOTIA

ATLANTIC OCEAN

QUÉBEC

Chibougamau

Québec

Montréal

Foxe Basin

Inukjuak

Kuujjuarapik

OTTAWA

Oshawa

Toronto

Matagami

Kirkland Lake

Sudbury

Coral Harbour

Chesterfield Inlet

Hudson Bay

Fort Severn

ONTARIO

Fort Albany

Moosonee

Somerset Island

Gioa Haven

Baker Lake

Arviat

Gillam

Norway House

Pine Dock

Kenora

Prince of Wales Island

Prince William Island

Brochet

Flin Flon

Grand Rapids

Dauphin

N U N A V U T   T E R R I T O R Y

Stony Rapids

MANITOBA

Kinoosao

Yorkton

Brandon

Banks Island

Victoria Island

Cambridge Bay

Bathurst Inlet

Reliance

Cluff Lake

La Loche

Meadow Lake

La Ronge

Prince Albert

SASKATCHEWAN

Regina

Holman

Kugluktuk

Echo Bay

Yellowknife

Pine Point

Peace Point

Sachs Harbour

Norman Wells

Fort Franklin

NORTHWEST TERRITORIES

Hay River

BEAUFORT SEA

Tuktoyaktuk

Fort Good Hope

Wrigley

Fort Simpson

Fort Liard

Fort Nelson

Dawson Creek

Grande Prairie

ALBERTA

Edmonton

Jasper

Calgary

Lethbridge

BRITISH COLUMBIA

Fort St. John

New Hazelton

Marilla

Bella Coola

Vancouver

Old Crow

YUKON TERRITORY

Dawson

Mayo

Beaver Creek

Whitehorse

Ross River

Watson Lake

Gulf of Alaska

A L A S K A   US

U N I T E D   S T A T E S

PACIFIC OCEAN

Legend

Ports/Harbors

Agriculture

Forestry

ECONOMIC FACT SHEET

GDP in U.S. Dollars: $923 billion

GDP Sectors: Services 69%, industry 29%, agriculture 2%

Land Use: Arable land 5%, other 95%

Currency: Canadian dollar (CAD); Canadian dollar per U.S. dollar: 1.6003

Workforce: Services 74%, manufacturing 15%, construction 5%, agriculture 3%, other 3%

Major Agricultural Products: Wheat, barley, oilseed, tobacco, fruits, vegetables, dairy products, forest products, fish

Major Exports: $274 billion—motor vehicles and parts, industrial machinery, aircraft, telecommunications equipment, chemicals, plastics, fertilizers, wood pulp, timber, crude petroleum, natural gas, electricity, aluminum

Major Imports: $239 billion—machinery and equipment, motor vehicles and parts, crude oil, chemicals, electricity, durable consumer goods

Significant Trading Partners:

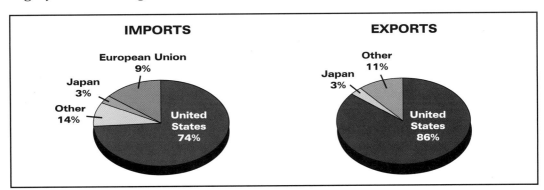

IMPORTS

European Union 9%

Japan 3%

Other 14%

United States 74%

EXPORTS

Other 11%

Japan 3%

United States 86%

Rate of Unemployment: 7.2%

Highways: 560,416 miles (901,902 km)

Railroads: 22,440 miles (36,114 km)

Waterways: 1,864 miles (3,000 km) (including St. Lawrence Seaway)

POLITICAL FACT SHEET

Official Country Name:
Canada

System of Government:
Confederation with
parliamentary democracy

Federal Structure:
Executive branch: chief of
state represented by
governor general (appointed
by the monarch on the
advice of the prime
minister). Head of govern-

ment: prime minister, deputy prime minister. Cabinet: federal ministry chosen
by the prime minister from among the members of his or her own party in
Parliament. Legislative branch: bicameral Parliament consisting of the Senate
and the House of Commons. Judicial branch: Supreme Court of Canada.

Number of Registered Voters: 19,906,796 (Eighteen years of age, universal)

National Anthem:
"O Canada" was adopted as Canada's national anthem on July 1, 1980, though
the song itself is a century old. Its music was composed by Calixa Lavallée,
and its original French lyrics were written by Sir Adolphe-Basile Routhier. The
English lyrics printed below were written in 1908 by Robert Stanley Weir.

O Canada! Our home and native land!
True patriot love in all thy sons command.
With glowing hearts we see thee rise,
The True North strong and free!
From far and wide, O Canada,
We stand on guard for thee.
God keep our land glorious and free!
O Canada, we stand on guard for thee.
O Canada, we stand on guard for thee.

CULTURAL FACT SHEET

Official Languages: English and French

Major Religions: Christianity, Buddhism, Sikhism, Hinduism, Judaism, and Islam

Capital: Ottawa

Population: 31.4 million

Ethnic Groups: European descent 85%, Asian 9%, Indigenous Indian and Inuit 2%, other 4%

Life Expectancy: 74 for males and 80.6 for females

Time: Greenwich Mean Time plus nine hours [GMT +0900]

Literacy Rate: 99%

National Symbol: Maple leaf

Cultural Leaders:

Visual Arts: Jack Bush, Emily Carr, Paul Kane, F. E. H. McDonald

Literature: Margaret Atwood, Saul Bellow, Arthur Hailey, Jack Kerouac, Stephen Leacock

Music: Bryan Adams, Paul Anka, Celine Dion, k.d. lang, Joni Mitchell, Neil Young

Entertainment: Genevieve Bujold, Raymond Burr, Michael J. Fox, Lorne Greene, Margot Kidder, Raymond Massey, Christopher Plummer, William Shatner, Donald Sutherland

Sports: Wayne Gretzky, Steve Nash, Bobby Orr

National Holidays and Festivals

New Year's Day: January 1
Good Friday and Easter: Dates for both vary according to the Christian calendar
Victoria Day: Monday before May 25
Canada Day: July 1

Labor Day: First Monday in September
Thanksgiving Day: Second Monday in October
Remembrance Day: November 11
Christmas: December 25
Boxing Day: December 26

Working Life: Forty-hour workweek from Monday through Friday, with two weeks off for vacation

GLOSSARY

Algonquin (al-GAHN-kwin) A major First Nation cultural group who first settled in the Great Lakes Region and now live throughout Canada, though predominantly in western regions.

Arctic Lowland (ARK-tic LOH-land) Also known as the tundra, it is a semi-frozen, treeless region located in northern Canada.

Beringia (beh-REN-gee-a) A landmass that once existed between Russia and Alaska. Asian explorers crossed it when they first entered North America approximately fifteen thousand years ago.

Canadian Shield (can-NAY-dee-in SHEELD) Formed more than two billion years ago during an ice age, it covers about half of mainland Canada and is characterized by its numerous rivers, lakes, and forests.

First Nations (FURST NAY-shunz) Descendants of Canada's first people, who came to North America via Beringia.

Front de Libération du Québec (FRONT deh lih-bayr-AH-see-yun do kay BEC) A political party that advocated Québec's secession from Canada during the 1970s.

Group of Seven (GROOP uv SEH-vin) An artists' organization that was formed in the early 1900s by a small group of landscape painters whose work had a modern theme.

Hudson Bay Lowlands (HUD-son BAY LOH-landz) A flat, swampy region located to the southwest of Hudson Bay.

Interior Plains (in-TEER-ee-or PLAYNZ) A region in central Canada characterized by flat land, much of which is used to grow a variety of grains. It is also known as Canada's breadbasket.

Inuit (IH-noo-wit) An Eskimo of North America and Greenland.

Iroquois (EER-ah-koy) A major First Nation cultural group who were found predominantly in Canada's southeastern regions. Though their numbers were greatly reduced by the arrival of the Europeans, they still live throughout Canada.

Métis (may-TEES) Canadian whose ethnic background is a mixture of French and First Nation.

Nunavut (NUN-ah-voot) A First Nations territory established in the 1990s located in the eastern Northwest Territories.

Ojibway (oh-JIB-way) A tribe of Algonquian-speaking North American Indians inhabiting regions of Canada and the United States around Lake Superior.

Painters Eleven (PAIN-turz ee-LEV-un) A group of artists who organized to increase the profile of abstract art in Canada.

Paleo-Indians (pay-lee-oh-IN-dee-ins) The first people to explore Canada, they arrived in North America approximately fifteen thousand years ago.

poutine (pooh-TEEN) A French Canadian food that combines French fries with a gravy and cheese.

Seven Years War (SEH-vin YEERZ WOR) A war that lasted from 1756 to 1763 and in which many powerful countries in Europe took part. This war included struggles between Great Britain and France about control of North America.

totem pole (TOH-tum pohl)   A wooden post that is carved and painted with a series of symbols and erected near a home. Totem poles have traditionally been made by First Nations living in Canada's northwestern coastal regions.

tourtiere (tor-tee-AYR)   A French meat pie that is often baked and eaten during Christmas celebrations.

tundra (TUN-drah)   A semifrozen region located in the Arctic that accounts for 20 percent of Canada's landmass.

Western Cordillera (WES-tern koor-dih-LAYR-ah)   A mountainous region in Canada located near Canada's west coast.

FOR MORE INFORMATION

The Embassy of Canada
501 Pennsylvania Avenue NW
Washington, DC 20001
(301) 782-1740
Web site: http://www.canadianembassy.org

Environment Canada
351 St. Joseph Boulevard
Hull, PQ K1A 0H3
Canada
(800) 668-6767
Web site: http://www.ec.gc.ca

Government of Canada Web Site
Communication Canada
Ottawa, ON K1A 1M4
Canada
Web site: http://www.canada.gc.ca/
    main_e.html

National Library of Canada
395 Wellington Street
Ottawa, ON K1A 0N4
Canada

Statistical Reference Centre
R.H. Coats Building, Lobby
Holland Avenue
Ottawa, ON K1A 0T6
Canada
(613) 951-8116
Web site: http: //www.statcan.ca

Web Sites

Due to the changing nature of Internet links, the Rosen Publishing Group, Inc., has developed an online list of Web sites related to the subject of this book. This site is updated regularly. Please use this link to access the list:

http://www.rosenlinks.com/pswc/cana

FOR FURTHER READING

Bothwell, Robert, Ian Drummond, and John English. *Canada since 1945: Power, Politics and Provincialism*. Toronto, ON: University of Toronto Press, 1989.

Bowers, Vivien, and Dianne Eastman. *Only in Canada: From the Colossal to the Kooky* (Wow Canada). Toronto, ON: Owl Books, 2002.

Brown, Craig. *The Illustrated History of Canada*. Toronto, ON: Lester & Orpen Dennys, 1998.

Englar, Mary. *The Iroquois: The Six Nations Confederacy*. Mankato, MN: Bridgestone Books, 2002.

Gentilcore, R. Louis, ed. *Historical Atlas of Canada, Volume 2: The Land Transformed, 1800–1891*. Toronto, ON: University of Toronto Press, 1993.

Hacker, Carlotta. *The Kids Book of Canadian History* (Kids Books). Toronto, ON: Kids Can Press, 2002.

Holmes, John W. *Life with Uncle: The Canadian-American Relationship*. Toronto, ON: University of Toronto Press, 1981.

Malcolm, Andrew H. *The Canadians*. Toronto, ON: Paperjacks, 1987.

Rogers, Barbara Radcliffe. *Canada* (Enchantment of the World Series). New York: Children's Press, 2002.

BIBLIOGRAPHY

Bumstead, J. M. *A History of the Canadian Peoples*. Don Mills, ON: Oxford University Press, 1998.

MacKay, Kathryn. *Discover Canada: Ontario*. Toronto, ON: Grolier Limited, 1996.

Malcolm, Andrew. *The Land and People of Canada*. New York: HarperCollins Publishers, 1991.

Marsh, James H, ed. *The Canadian Encyclopedia 2000*. Toronto, ON: McClelland & Stewart, 2000.

Riendeau, Roger. *A Brief History of Canada*. New York: Facts on File, Inc., 2000.

See, Scott, W. *The History of Canada*. Westport, CT: Greenwood Press, 2001.

PRIMARY SOURCE IMAGE LIST

Page 22: The Algonquin petroglyphs in this photograph date between 500 and 1,000 years ago and are located in Ontario, Canada.

Page 23: The fossil in this photograph is located at Miguasha Park in Québec, Canada.

Page 25: This image was taken from the *Travels of Sir John Ross* and is located at the Navy Historical Service in Vincennes, France.

Page 26: *Discovery of America* by Leif Eriksson is a nineteenth-century painting located at the Library of Congress in Washington, D.C.

Page 27: This map of Canada showing the St. Lawrence River dates from 1536.

Page 28 (top): This portrait of Jacques Cartier was painted in 1545.

Page 29 (top): This map of Hochelaga (present-day Montréal) in New France was published in Venice, Italy, between 1556 and 1606 and is located at the Bibliothèque des Arts Décoratifs in Paris, France.

Page 29 (bottom): This illustration depicts the capture of Québec in 1759 and dates from that same year.

Page 33 (bottom): This photograph of Donald A. Smith, First Baron Strathcona and Mount Royal, shows him driving the last spike at Craigellachie, British Columbia, on November 7, 1885.

Page 34 (top): Sir Wilfred Laurier, the first French Canadian prime minister, is pictured in this historic photograph taken by G. Vandyk in 1901.

Page 34 (bottom): This poster from World War II is located in the World War II Museum in Paris, France.

Page 35 (top): Canada's twelfth prime minister, Louis Saint Laurent, who served from 1948 to 1957, is pictured in this historic photograph taken in the 1950s.

Page 35 (bottom): Canadian troops and German prisoners are pictured in this photograph taken at the Battle of Arras by William C. Shrout, in September 1918. It is now located at the Imperial War Museum in London, England.

Page 36: Queen Elizabeth II and Canadian prime minister Pierre Trudeau are pictured in this photograph taken during the signing of the constitution of 1982 on April 17, 1982. This image is now a part of the collection located at the National Archives in Ottawa, Canada.

Page 44: Willie Seaweed carved the memorial pole seen in this photograph in 1931 in Alert Bay, Canada.

Page 50: This photograph of a Haida Indian village dates from 1900.

Page 61: This sixteenth-century illustration titled *Cartier Takes Possession of New France* marks the arrival of Catholicism and was created by W. Croome.

Page 62 (top): This eighteenth-century engraving by J. M. Dumesnil shows Europeans and missionaries arriving in Canada and is part of a private collection.

Page 62 (bottom): The baptism of Indians at Port Royal in Nova Scotia. This illustration dates from 1600.

Page 63: This is an undated portrait of Joseph Brant, a Mohawk Indian chief who established the first Episcopal Church in Canada.

Page 64: The oil painting shown here was created by Canadian artist Paul Kane and is dated 1849. It is located at the Royal Ontario Museum in Toronto, Canada.

Page 72: The totem poles in this photograph were made by the Northwest Indians and are located in Stanley Park in Vancouver, Canada.

Page 74: Created by the Inuit, this soapstone carving is undated.

Page 75: Canada's Parliament buildings on Parliament Hill were constructed in 1866 are located in Ottawa, Canada.

Page 83: Samuel de Champlain's manuscript, an account of his search for the Northwest Passage and his travels in New France, *Les Voyages de la Novvelle France*, was written in 1629.

Page 84: This photograph of Margaret Atwood was taken in August 2001.

Page 85: This photograph of Mordecai Richler was taken in Montréal in 1992.

Page 87: This photograph of Robert Charlebois was taken in May 2000.

Page 90: This photograph of Alanis Morissette was taken in June 2001.

Page 91: This photograph of Celine Dion was taken in 1996.

INDEX

Canada: A Primary Source Cultural Guide

About the Author

Lois Sakany is a freelance writer living in Brooklyn, New York.

Designer: Geri Fletcher; **Cover Designer:** Tahara Hasan; **Editor:** Joann Jovinelly;
Photo Researcher: Gillian Harper; **Photo Research Assistant:** Fernanda Rocha